50 WAYS TO SUPPORT YOUR CHILD'S

From **IEPs** to **Assorted Therapies,** an Empowering Guide to Taking Action, Every Day

SPECIAL EDUCATION

TERRI MAURO

Avon, Massachusetts

Published by
Adams Media, a division of F+W Media, Inc.
57 Littlefield Street, Avon, MA 02322. U.S.A.
www.adamsmedia.com

ISBN 10: 1-60550-112-3
ISBN 13: 978-1-60550-112-3
Printed in the United States of America.

J   I   H   G   F   E   D   C   B   A

Library of Congress Cataloging-in-Publication Data
is available from the publisher.

This publication is designed to provide accurate and authoritative information
with regard to the subject matter covered. It is sold with the understanding that
the publisher is not engaged in rendering legal, accounting, or other professional
advice. If legal advice or other expert assistance is required, the services of a com-
petent professional person should be sought.

—From a *Declaration of Principles* jointly adopted by a Committee of the
American Bar Association and a Committee of Publishers and Associations

Many of the designations used by manufacturers and sellers to distinguish their
product are claimed as trademarks. Where those designations appear in this book
and Adams Media was aware of a trademark claim, the designations have been
printed with initial capital letters.

This book is available at quantity discounts for bulk purchases.
For information, please call 1-800-289-0963.

To Elena and Andrew,
for whom I learned these lessons;
and to Rick,
for always holding down the fort.

Contents

Introduction

Most books on special education focus on Individualized Education Plans (IEPs)—helping parents learn the laws that govern IEPs and how to wield those laws strategically in meetings with school personnel. That's important, and there will always be times when battles are necessary and unavoidable.

But IEP planning and enforcement aren't the only ways to help your child have a strong special-education experience. Involving yourself in your child's education is important, too. There are many, many things you can do that will make a difference.

Ultimately, they may empower you to become more involved in the IEP process. And if you are already doing battle on that front, these fifty things can help you improve your platform for advocacy and engage in some positive interactions with school personnel.

Some of the fifty things to do in this book simply involve changes in your home routine. Others require interaction with teachers and therapists and caseworkers, and a few do deal specifically with those dreaded IEPs. All of them can empower you to be a part of your child's special-education team, whether you're just providing background support or actively working for change.

Many of these are things that parents of children in regular education do every day. They may be harder for you because your child is not at your neighborhood school, taking a bus to a place you rarely see. They may be harder because you are juggling so many other challenges and heartaches. They may be harder because you feel unequipped to educate your challenged child or to interact with educators who make you feel ignorant.

Still, among these fifty things, there will be at least one that you can do easily. Start with that. Then add another. Set modest goals. Anything is better than nothing. You are an important part of your child's special-education team. You are the expert on your child. All the small things you do can add up to a big change. As we know from watching our kids grow, little things mean a lot.

THE

WAYS

1 Give Your Child a Calm Start to the Day

As parents, we tend to focus on what the school is going to do for our children. How will they maximize learning potential? How will they handle behavior problems? It's a powerless feeling to know how important what goes on in that building is to your child, and how distant you are from the proceedings.

As it happens, though, you do have one very important power, and that's the power to get your child to school in the morning calm, rested, and ready to learn.

It's the duty of every parent, really, but all the more vital for parents of children in special education. Our kids are so much more likely to experience major stress during the school day—from learning struggles or physical discomfort to social conflicts or behavior control—than their regular-education peers. If there's a load of family discord on their young shoulders, too, the way will be that much harder.

In his book *Kids in the Syndrome Mix of ADHD, LD, Asperger's, Tourette's, Bipolar and More*, pediatric neurologist Martin L. Kutscher suggests thinking of your child as having a stress speedometer; when the needle passes sixty, there's going to be a meltdown. Things that happen during the day push that needle up, up, up toward the danger zone. Your child's a lot more likely to hit that bad patch if you start him out at fifty-nine.

Think about how mornings go at your house. Identify the things that cause your child distress—getting up early? uncomfortable clothes? food that's not a favorite? scattered backpack contents? bed-making? angry parental nagging?—and change them.

Easier said than done? Sure. But doable, and worth doing.

The beauty of morning routines is that they're a "whatever works" situation. Getting through that A.M. rush peaceably is such a high priority that all other rules and requirements can go out the window. This is not a time to argue with your child about what clothes she'll wear or what foods he'll agree to eat. Offer choices of mutually acceptable apparel. Serve whatever odd breakfast your child will consume (for my son, it's often leftovers from the night before). Getting your child out of the house clothed, fed, and calm is more important than dressing her like a fashion plate or fixing a gourmet breakfast.

If organization is the problem, check the book bag the night before and make sure everything's in order. If early rising is hard, do absolutely everything the night before—including sleeping in sweats or a T-shirt that can be worn to school. Should you be lucky enough to have an early rising child in your family, try putting that sibling in charge of waking all the sleepyheads up (including you, if necessary).

Getting your child to school in the morning with as clean a slate as possible is a way to support your child's special education that involves no meetings, no research, no interactions with school personnel, just a change in the way you do things. And as a bonus, you'll get a fresher start on the morning, too.

Five Good Reasons to Do It

1. It shows respect for school and the work your child does there.
2. Your child will be more likely to succeed and reach goals.
3. Good mornings are a positive experience for the whole family.
4. You'll start the day feeling in control of your child.
5. It's a way to make a noticeable improvement in your child's school day that's entirely under your control.

Three Bad Reasons Not To

1. **School behavior is the school's problem.** Unfortunately, what happens at school doesn't stay at school. It comes back to you in the form of notes and disciplinary warnings and Saturday detentions and wimpy IEP goals. Better to keep the bad from happening in the first place than to deal with the consequences.

2. **Something always goes wrong in the morning no matter what.** Okay. So make your goal for one *fewer* thing to go wrong. Every little bit helps.

3. **I'm not a morning person.** You and me both. If mornings are your worst time, too, all the more reason to get pretty much everything but breakfast done the night before. Make a project of it with your child, as mutual morning grumps.

Keep In Mind

Sometimes, the morning race is in pursuit of that early, early school-bus pickup. Ask yourself how much stress that adds to your mornings—and if the answer is, "A lot," think about whether you might be able to do the school transport yourself. A little extra time at home, plus a little talk time in the car, can provide a welcome morning boost for some kids. Assuming, of course, that you're not speeding and swearing and yelling at other drivers all the way.

2 Make Sure Your Child Gets Enough Sleep

Once a year or so, whenever standardized testing rolls around in your school district, you probably get that note, the one that asks you to make sure your child gets adequate rest every school night. The school knows that students need to be well-rested and alert for the hard work of filling in bubbles on a piece of paper.

But school is hard work for your child every day of the year. For students in special education, most schoolwork is as challenging as those all-important test questions. Just sitting at a desk or maneuvering a pencil can be a test of will. So why not keep that rest regimen up all through the school year?

It's one of the great contradictions of parenting that children who haven't slept enough often show their rest deficit in overactivity. You'd think they'd just drop where they stand, but nope—they jump, they dance, they scram, they scream. That's hard enough to handle at home, but in a classroom where a certain degree of decorum is required, it's a disaster.

Enforcing bedtime is necessary, then, but it's certainly not easy. You can put the child to bed, but you can't make him sleep. Still, developing a bedtime routine, with a calm period free of electronic devices before the hoped-for sleep time, is a good place to begin.

Two books worth looking at for suggestions on the hows, whys, and how muches of sleep for children are *Sleepless in America: Is Your Child Misbehaving or Missing Sleep?* by Mary Sheedy Kurcinka and *The Floppy Sleep Game Book: A Proven Four-Week Plan to Get Your Child to Sleep* by Patti Teel.

How much sleep is enough? That's going to vary from child to child, but generally, experts recommend ten to twelve hours for school-age children, and nine hours for teens. Figure out the latest your child can sleep and still have a calm morning routine, and then count backwards. You may be surprised by how early in the evening your little one should be hitting the pillow. If your evenings are a swirl of activity—aftercare, homework, sports, lessons, therapy, TV, late dinner, late bedtime—you may have to do some serious restructuring to get all that sleep in.

Do it. Sleep is the base on which the pyramid of your child's life has to rest, and if it's full of holes, the whole structure is going to be shaky. Plan your afternoons and evenings accordingly.

While you're looking at the things that keep your child from getting enough sleep, consider the amount of sleep you're getting, too. Just as lack of sleep can make your child hyper and hard to handle, it can make you impatient and inflexible. Sufficient shut-eye for you can pay off in a less-tense child, too. (Put down this book and go to bed!)

Five Good Reasons to Do It

1. Adequate sleep will pay off for your child at school and at home.

2. It's a good excuse for cutting down on activities you know are out of control.

3. Bedtime routines create some good bonding time for you and your child.

4. Earlier bedtimes give you some much-needed, child-free downtime, too.

5. You get to feel all smug and superior to those other parents when the "rest up for testing!" notices go out.

Three Bad Reasons Not To

1. **My child refuses to go to bed.** You can't force your child to sleep, but you can make the alternative so boring that sleep will be an attractive option. Put the computer to bed, the iPod to bed, the TV to bed, the stereo to bed, the toys to bed, and the light bulb to bed. If your child wishes to stay awake staring at the dark walls, at least that's restful.

2. **My child stays up late with hours of homework.** Homework's important, but it shouldn't be keeping your child up at night. See if there's an opportunity to start work earlier, break it up into small bits, or otherwise complete it before

bedtime. If not, talk to the teacher about cutting it down or allowing some of the work to be done on weekends.

3. **There's absolutely nothing we can cut from our schedule.** How about *one thing*? Start small. Find an extra fifteen minutes. Work from there.

Keep In Mind

Is it a favorite TV show that's keeping you or your child awake? Invest in a digital video recorder, and those slept-through shows will be available for watching during more reasonable hours. They can even be motivators for getting your child going in the morning: Watching a recording of that missed program can be a reward for getting up, dressed, fed, bed made, and book bag ready with time to spare.

3   Go Through Your Child's Book Bag Daily

It may look like just a bunch of folders and books and papers to you, but the contents of your child's book bag can tell you a lot about just what's going on in that long day away from you during the schoolday.

If the bag is well-organized, with everything in its place, it will be easy to flip through and see what's being studied. You can check that notes are being taken adequately, see what test grades have been given, update yourself on what your child's supposed to be studying, and identify trouble spots to discuss with the teacher at the next conference.

If the bag contains permission slips or report cards or important notices, you'll want to get them right away, and not when your child suddenly recalls their existence, or the teacher calls to ask why you haven't responded.

If the bag is mostly empty, you'll want to check with the teacher to make sure that it's *supposed* to be—is your child forgetting to bring things home? Is his locker a complete disastrous mess, jammed full of things that are supposed to be traveling with him? Or is all work being done and kept at school on purpose, and if so, hey, how's that kid doing, anyway?

Finally, if it's the *bag* that's a complete disastrous mess, you'll know that your child has a problem with organization that's probably impacting her school performance, and nobody is taking any pains to help with it.

Go ahead and take those pains yourself. Organize that bag. Create a system to put papers in their place, and then go through the bag again every night to re-sort and reorganize. Certainly, your child is the one who should be doing this. And certainly, you'd hope that somebody at school would be working on that. But, in the meantime, until both of those things happen? There's no reason your child should have to suffer the consequences of being unable to sort papers and maintain order.

You can make it a routine to sift through that sack with your child every day after school, or work together to organize it after homework time. Take a peek while you're marking time in a waiting room anticipating the end of a lesson or therapy session, or after your child goes to bed. But know what's in that bag. It's a great way to make sure that important things don't fall through the cracks—or, more accurately, get lost in the debris.

Plus, between us: Sometimes you'll find candy in that book bag that some kindly aide or therapist has given as a reward, and your child has forgotten. You'll want to selflessly eat that to save your child from weight gain and tooth decay.

Five Good Reasons to Do It

1. You'll be more likely to receive teacher notes and school notices.
2. It will help you understand where your child is struggling.
3. It will help you understand where your child is succeeding, too.
4. Your child will know you're interested in what's going on at school.
5. Going through book-bag stuff can be a nice bonding time with your child.

Three Bad Reasons Not To

1. **It's a violation of my child's privacy.** Not if you let your child know you're going to do it. Some storage places are just plain public domain. That drawer in the kitchen. The dining room table. The back seat of the car. And, yes, your child's book bag. Whatever's there is fair game, if you've given fair warning. Of course, if your child still protests, then you'll have to start to wonder what's so important to keep hidden.

2. **I don't know what to keep or what to throw away.** Don't focus on cleaning out in your foraging expeditions so much as sorting out. If there's any chance the massive wad of crumpled papers contains something that needs to be

turned in or studied, put it in a folder. Color-code the folders by class, and have your child help you divide and conquer. Pass on good packrat coping strategies now.

3. **My child has the book bag under control.** Great! How about taking a daily opportunity to admire that organizational handiwork and compliment the painstaking orderliness? And then, maybe, set those impressive clutter-wrangling skills loose on that kitchen drawer.

Keep In Mind

If your child is strongly resistant to you rifling through the book bag, or there's never enough time to do that sort of search mission justice, consider providing a see-through plastic backpack. Many schools are requiring these to cut down on the bringing of forbidden objects to school, and you can just as well require them to cut down on the bringing of unimaginably unkempt book bags to school. And to locate moldy gym clothes.

4 Memorize Your Child's Schedule

It's the middle of the school day. Do you know where your child is?

If the hours your student spends on that campus is a big blur of undifferentiated school time to you, get a copy of his or her schedule and study it.

Don't have one at hand? Make your own. Your school district most likely has a website that includes a copy of the bell schedule for whatever level of school your child is at. Print it out, and then make it a little project to sit with your child and find out what happens each period. If communication of this sort isn't your little one's strong suit, you may be able to get the same information from a report card or a guidance counselor.

When a schedule of therapy times comes home at the start of the year, pencil those in on your makeshift schedule as well.

Having a good idea of your child's daily routine can pay off in all sorts of ways. If there's a problem, you're perfectly positioned to interpret it according to what is going on when it happens, just as you would be with behavioral flare-ups at home. If grades or self-control slip in a subject that's right before or after lunch, or at the end of the day, or in a period often interrupted by therapy sessions, you'll have a place to begin the conversation.

If your child spends the day with the same teacher, there's likely one period—maybe gym, art, or music—in which another instructor takes charge. That's probably the classroom teacher's break period, and the portion of the day in which communications can most easily be exchanged. It's the time to call if you need to talk, and the time the teacher will call you if there's a problem. In addition, it's the most likely scheduling block for IEP meetings, when that time rolls around.

Back to that not-so-communicative child, your questions about school can be much more precise when you know the basic shape and routine of the school day. Ask specific questions about different subjects or routines. Kids sometimes feel that school is a zone in which parents do not exist or have any awareness about. Creating a connection to that time when you and your child are not together can strengthen your bond, and open the door to stories that might not otherwise emerge.

That bond goes both ways. Think about your child during the day. Send out good thoughts during the time of day you know there's a big test, or a challenging activity. It's easy to feel disconnected when your child takes a bus to a school outside your neighborhood, yet with a little effort, you can plug yourself back into that school day. It's a small gesture, but a powerful one.

Five Good Reasons to Do It

1. You're an expert on your child, and that should include the hours you're apart.
2. Knowing the schedule IDs you as an involved parent.
3. You'll be in a better position to pinpoint problems.
4. It helps you imagine what your child is up to.
5. It's one small easy thing you can do all by yourself.

Three Bad Reasons Not To

1. **That's the one part of the day I don't have to know what my child's doing.** Yeah, it may feel like a relief to not have to micromanage for six hours out of the day. But you can't disengage totally—your child needs you to stay aware 24/7. Not active, just aware. And interested, for sure.
2. **They keep changing the schedule anyway.** That happens, and you'll need to alert the school that such disruptions of routine will have an impact on your child's behavior and learning ability. It's hard to do that effectively if you don't know what the routine was supposed to be in the first place.
3. **The school doesn't want me to be involved.** Most schools do indeed want parents to be aware and supportive and informed—just not all up in the administration's face about

it. However, if your child's school is really actively resistant about letting you know what's going on when, that's all the more reason to find out. What exactly are they hiding?

Keep In Mind

Elementary-school teachers often rearrange the timing of subjects depending on what goes on during the day—a fire drill, an assembly, a classroom visitor. That's fine for the majority of students, but not for those who are pulled out during a particular subject for resource-room instruction. The pull-out time will stay the same, causing your child to miss one subject and get another one twice. Knowing the way the schedule's supposed to be can alert you to these mix-ups.

5   Ask Your Child Three Questions Every Day

Does this conversation sound familiar?

> **You**: *Honey, how was your day?*
> **Your Child**: *Fine.*

Not the most satisfying exchange of information, is it? But good luck getting much more than that if you ask general, nonspecific, brief-answer-permitting questions of kids for whom putting the events of the day into verbal form is a confusing, overwhelming, or even painful task. Instead of a boring open-ended question, or ones that allow a yes-or-no answer, try to be very specific in your after-school queries. Instead of "How was your day?" ask:

> *What did you eat for lunch?*
> *What did [name of classmate] have for lunch?*
> *Was anybody absent in your class today?*
> *Who got into trouble today?*
> *What did you play in gym?*
> *What did you play at recess?*

The more detailed or open-ended or goofy you can make your questions, the more likely you are to get something other than a grunt in response. As your discussions of school become richer, you can pluck information from one day's description and use it to inspire new questions. If one classmate always gets in trouble, or makes your child laugh, or often takes sick days, or orders the same lunch, or wears strange outfits, make sure to ask for a daily update of that youngster's activities.

One alternative to asking three questions is to tell your child to give you three answers. Give a nice reward after your child follows instructions to tell you three things that happened today, or three funny things, three scary things, three good things, three silly things. This approach is open-ended enough to accommodate all the various things that might happen in school, but not so open-ended that your child will drown in it.

In his book *The Pressured Child: Helping Your Child Find Success in School and Life,* child psychologist Michael Thompson suggests asking kids about how school *feels* for them, what their experience of school is, and that's another approach to take with a less-than-communicative kid. You may be surprised by what you find out. When I tried this sort of inquiry with my middle-school-age daughter, she burst into tears. Basic questions of how school *was* hadn't tapped into the anxiety that was overwhelming her, but these questions did. As a result, I was able to adjust her schedule in a way that made school less stressful and more productive.

If you take yourself out of the conversation, you'll never be able to make that kind of difference. Your child needs to know that you're truly, deeply interested in knowing what's going on: the good stuff and the bad stuff. And being in the know is empowering for you, too. When you're having a teacher conference or an IEP meeting and a certain issue comes up, instead of being blindsided you can say, "Oh, yes, my child mentioned that to me." And have something useful to say about it.

Five Good Reasons to Do It

1. As the expert on your child, you need that child's-eye view.
2. Kids may not act like it, but they like to know parents are interested.
3. It helps you address problems as soon as possible.
4. Talking boosts kids' language skills.
5. Hey, you're *curious*, aren't you?

Three Bad Reasons Not To

1. **My child never tells me anything.** It's frustrating to keep making advances that get shot down. But you're the grown-up here—it's your job to find some way to get a response

from that secretive son or daughter. Bribery is not out of the question.

2. **The teacher writes notes to tell me what's going on.** That's great! Information from the teacher makes an excellent starting point for conversations with your child and can help you ask better questions. But it doesn't replace those conversations. You'll want to get all points of view.

3. **I'm not sure I want to know what happened at school.** As much as we seek that connection, sometimes what we hear is not so fun. It would be nice to not have to know about the bully, the aide's inappropriate comment, the punishment administered by the teacher, or the disruptions of routine. But your child needs to talk about it, and you need to hear it.

Keep In Mind

Just as you're interested in your child's day, your child may be interested in what you've been doing, too. Make a game of it, answering one question in return for each one your child answers. The more back-and-forth exchanges the two of you can have, with questions being asked and answered, the richer your child's communication skills will become. Think of things throughout the day that might be of particular interest to your child, and tuck them away for future chatting.

6   Eavesdrop on Your Child's Play Time

You know who has been my most reliable source of information about my son's special-education classroom?

Not him. Not his teacher. Not his aide.

It's his imaginary friend.

He and Scooby, that unseen pal, have quite the conversations about school issues. If I press my ear against the door of his room and listen in, I can hear Scooby lecturing him on all manner of schoolyard happenings—often, from the sound of it, in the exact words and tone of his teacher. Little do the adults in his classroom know that I'm sending a recording device into their midst each and every day.

Sometimes I don't even have to eavesdrop to get the scoop from Scooby, because he comes right on up and tells me himself. That dog's kind of a tattletale.

But if your child doesn't have such an agreeable invisible companion, you can still learn lots from listening in at play time. Children will often act out issues that affect them emotionally as part of pretend play, so if you hear dolls lecturing other dolls, or toy cars bullying each other at intersections, give a listen to what they're going on about. You may hear scenarios from school being repeated, processed, and responded to.

Playing school with your child is another fun way to get the scoop. Volunteer to be your child's student, and notice the way she conducts the class. If there are situations you're curious about, act them out and see how he reacts. Sometimes you'll be treated to a fairly exact re-enactment of incidents that have occurred in class. At other times, you may get a general sense of what stresses your child out, what she gets preoccupied by, and what areas you may want to discuss with the teacher.

If creative play isn't your child's particular thing, you still have options for interpretation of leisure activities. Say what you will about children's TV shows, they're generally rich in school situations that can form the basis of a conversation. Watch those programs with your child, and ask your young viewing companion—during commercials, or after the show is over—whether he's ever faced a similar situation, or what she thinks the character in question should do. Use those shared viewing situations as points of reference for future conversations about school.

The same, of course, is true of children's literature, which is often so full of schoolyard slights and tragedies that the books are tough for parents to read. Still, if your child has a strong interest in reading and you have a strong heart for tugging, sit and read together and discuss all those Scary Bad Things. Your child may have insights that can clue you in to his own school-day traumas.

And you'll learn how not to be a clueless parent like so many of those kid-lit Moms and Dads.

Five Good Reasons to Do It

1. You can spy on school without ever leaving your house.
2. Watching your child play can clue you into developmental factors, too.
3. Playing more with your kid is something you should be doing anyway.
4. TV viewing or reading makes for fairly effortless together-time.
5. It's almost always good for a laugh, and who couldn't use that?

Three Bad Reasons Not To

1. **I'm not around when my child plays.** Your child may do most of his playing in day care or before you get home from work, but create a little space for play during the time you're together—on a weekend, if not on weekdays. There's too much to be learned, for both of you, to let the chance go to waste.
2. **My child doesn't play.** It may not look like what you'd consider playing, but what we're talking about here is how your child fills his leisure time. Whether he's talking to himself or

to his imaginary friend or to his endless line-up of cars, the stresses of the day are likely to show through.

3. **I'd just be jumping to conclusions.** Better jumped-to conclusions than none at all. You're not going to run to the principal in a rage because of something your child said to her teddy bear. But you're going to make a note of it, and let it inform your conversations with school personnel.

Keep In Mind

You know how your child repeats things that the teacher said in school? Here's a chilling fact for you: He probably does the same thing at school with the words that you say. Take it from one who's learned the hard way: You need to be careful what you say about schools and teachers while your child is in earshot. Those same imaginary friends who tell all to you will turn right around and sell you out.

7   Make Sure the Teacher Has All Your Contact Information

You know it's the start of a new school year when that enormous packet of papers comes home for you to fill out. Again and again, you're asked to provide your home phone, work phone, cell phone, fax phone, friend's phone, relative's phone, doctor's phone, enough phone numbers to fill a directory and give yourself serious hand cramps.

The sheets will probably indicate that this information is in case of emergency, and certainly, should an emergency occur, you'll want the school to be able to contact you.

But there are plenty of other reasons the school may want to get in touch—some worrisome, some productive, some downright pleasant. Ensuring that you're fully available at all times and for all situations is an important part of supporting your child's special education.

During the years my children were in middle school, I often volunteered in the media center, at the front desk by the phone the teachers had to use to call parents. Over and over, I heard them complain of phone numbers that didn't work, work numbers that reached the wrong person, messages that were never returned.

These teachers were calling to alert parents to upcoming tests, to warn of imminent grade peril, to arrange after-school assistance for a struggling student, or to make sure that word of a project or assignment had made it home. But all too often, those helpful efforts were defeated by a lack of availability by the parent.

We're a mobile society. We change jobs. We change cell-phone providers. We move around. Phone numbers change. It happens. But when it does, be absolutely sure that your child's school—*all* your children's schools—get the update. You might want to keep a copy of that information form taped in your child's communication notebook so it's easy to change, or at least stash one in the folder where you keep your child's school records so you'll remember what you filled out the last time.

And while you're at it, give the information not only to the school office but directly to your child's teacher. From the start of the year, make sure the teacher or teachers know all the ins and outs of getting in touch with you, where you are when and how you can be found. Chances are, teachers will try to get in touch during their break period—and if you followed the advice about learning your child's school schedule, you know when that is—or directly after school. Make it clear when you can be reached during those times, and if those times are impossible, which times you would prefer.

Lately, e-mail is becoming a good way for parents and teachers to stay in touch. Ask the teacher if you can exchange e-mail addresses, and then you can keep in contact without worrying about timing or missed connections. Two things to keep in mind, though: If a teacher e-mails you and needs a reply, return that message promptly—which means monitoring your e-mail closely. And on your end, don't abuse your access, constantly peppering the teacher with questions and complaints and concerns and requests. It's a good way to get your e-mails sent to the spam folder.

Five Good Reasons to Do It

1. You'll be available in case of emergency.
2. You'll be available in case of classroom problems.
3. You'll be available in case of an adorable anecdote.
4. You won't have to rely on your child for last-minute information.
5. You'll know how to reach that teacher right back, too.

Three Bad Reasons Not To

1. **I can't take calls at work.** That's a legitimate concern, but in that case, you need to be even clearer with the school about when you can be reached with nonemergencies and who needs to be called if an emergency happens. Don't leave them with no options at all.

2. **My child knows how to get in touch with me.** Great! That means any calls that will be taking place while your child is conscious and present in school are A-OK, and so are any calls to which your child can be an ear-witness. If the teacher wants to talk after school or on a sick day, though, or hoped to speak to the parent without the student knowing, making your child the Keeper of the Number is a pretty ineffective method. Let the school know, too.

3. **The school should keep better track of numbers.** Yeah, it's frustrating that, in this day and age, you still have to keep filling out those papers and cards and telling each individual individually. It is what it is. Your need to be available is greater than your need to vent your frustration on this particular matter.

Keep In Mind

Many schools have put together websites to keep students and parents up-to-date on assignments. Ask if your teacher has such a web presence, and use the site as a way to keep up and keep in touch. Let the teacher know if you find it useful.

8   Correspond with Your Child's Teacher

There are all kinds of ways to keep in touch with the school. Having all your contact information up-to-date so phone calls can be made, as we discussed in the previous chapter, is one way. Another is to keep up a pleasant correspondence with the teacher, through informal notes back and forth.

Griping and complaining to your spouse and friends and hoping that somehow the universe will convey your concerns to the one who needs to hear them? Not very effective at all.

Often, particularly in the early elementary grades, teachers will provide a communication notebook to serve as a link between home and school. If one of these rides in your child's book bag, be sure to check it daily for notes, and add to it regularly yourself. Share things you've noticed while helping with homework, strategies that have been useful in handling behavior, stresses at home that may be affecting your child's school demeanor, and any other information you think the teacher might find useful.

When you have no such formal format for your correspondence, though, sliding a note in a school folder is a perfectly acceptable way of sharing your insights. Homework is a particularly good subject to write about. If you notice your child is struggling or you provide extensive assistance or the work takes an excessive amount of time or you've found a way of working that helped your child, jot that information down and clip the note to the homework sheet. Teachers don't really send all that homework home to make you miserable—they do it to reinforce skills and check ability. Anything that impacts on that, they need to know about.

Not every note has to express a complaint or a concern or a problem. Think about how much you enjoyed hearing the story of some small triumph or charming moment in your child's school day. If your young student is doing something adorable at home that reflects school experiences, send the teacher a note about it.

Similarly, you may have appreciated the way information from school gives you an "in" for starting conversations with your child. Provide that same service for teachers by writing in about special occurrences in your child's life. You'll help the teacher get a conversation going and give your child a chance to shine.

Depending on the school or your particular relationship with the administration, there may be restrictions limiting your communication. Paraprofessionals are often forbidden to correspond with parents, and your notes to the teacher may have to travel through official channels, with responses requiring the approval of the principal. That sort of thing can make you feel defensive and annoyed, but don't let it make you stop writing. It shows that you're a concerned parent, and the rest is just noise.

Five Good Reasons to Do It

1. You look like a concerned, involved parent.

2. Prompt exchange of ideas and information benefits everyone.

3. Your correspondence keeps your child foremost in the teacher's thoughts.

4. Meetings move more quickly when you don't have months of concerns saved up.

5. Keep copies of your notes, and you'll have a good record of issues from throughout the year.

Three Bad Reasons Not To

1. **I always forget to write.** Don't leave notes until the morning rush. Write them the night before or while your child is doing homework. Get a notepad with your name on the top, and keep it in the kitchen or wherever you're most likely to see it. You don't have to write a book—usually a few quick sentences will do.

2. **I'd rather talk to the teacher in person.** You certainly should be doing that, too, no doubt about it. But some things aren't big enough for a meeting or urgent enough for a phone call. Sending them in a note gets them off your mind and into the teacher's.

3. **Nobody ever reads what I write.** Well, they probably read it. What they don't do is respond, and there can be lots of reasons for that. All you can control is what you do, and writing notes—short, pleasant ones—is worth doing. Keep copies for your records, so you have proof that you, at least, made the effort.

Keep In Mind

Notes or communication books are also useful ways to keep in touch with the therapists who work with your child. Ask the therapist to make a note in the book every time he or she sees your child—and ask the teacher to make a note when a session is missed. In addition to keeping the lines of communication open, you'll find out if there's a major gap in services, and know what to ask for in terms of makeups.

9   Meet with Your Child's Teacher

Notes are good. So are phone calls and e-mails and exchanges on website message boards. But sometimes, there are things you really need to discuss with a teacher face to face. Sometimes, just showing your face is enough.

Most likely, your school has scheduled times for parent-teacher meetings. This may include a back-to-school night at the beginning of the year, and conference times around the release of progress reports and report cards.

These are great opportunities for informal contact and conversation with your child's teacher. You'll want to attend them if your child is having a problem, of course—particularly if you've been summoned—but even if everything's going smoothly, show up anyway. There are always things to talk about, and should the chat just circle around what a great kid you have and how well she's doing, why would you want to miss that?

Back-to-school night is a particularly good opportunity to meet not just the teacher but the paraprofessionals who work in your child's classroom. Seeing where your child spends his time and meeting the other parents can greatly increase your ability to talk with your child about her day, set up play dates with other students, and network about homework or other classroom issues.

If you can't make that annual event, and scheduled conference times don't fit in with your schedule, ask the teacher to set up another time to meet. This can be difficult when the teacher is only available during school hours and you're only available outside of them, but it's worth taking the occasional long lunch or morning off to have these friendly face-offs. Teachers are more willing to make an effort with your student when they know you're willing to make an effort, too.

Personal meetings accomplish things that more remote contact can't. When you can actually see facial expressions and hear tone of voice and follow the conversation in spontaneous directions, you're much less likely to have misunderstandings and more likely to forge a productive relationship. If you've seen that teacher a few times before facing off over an IEP table, you'll have anecdotes and conversations in common that can make such planning sessions less threatening.

Of course, after a personal meeting or two, you may come to the conclusion that you can't stand this teacher or the teacher can't stand you. That's useful information, too, and will inform the way you receive and process your child's complaints. Occasionally, you may need to request a change of teacher, if it's clear that this one doesn't suit your child's special needs. Hard to know that if you have only your child's poorly communicated word to go by.

Five Good Reasons to Do It

1. You look like a concerned, involved parent.
2. You get a good look at the teacher.
3. You'll probably meet in the classroom, so you get a good look at that, too.
4. It's a chance to form a relationship with the teacher that may benefit your child.
5. It's a chance to find out if the teacher is really as bad as your child says.

Three Bad Reasons Not To

1. **I can't take time off work.** Well, if you say so. Often, though, it's a matter of making your child's education a priority. If you'd take a few hours off to get your car repaired or go to a doctor's appointment, you can probably do so to make a meeting with your child's teacher. You don't have to do it a lot, but once in a while, you have to give this its due importance.
2. **I don't have transportation.** If you can walk to your other kids' school but your special-education child's campus is too far away, ask a friend for a ride. Check the bus schedule. Take a cab. Unless that school's in Timbuktu, you can get there—again, you just have to recognize it as a priority.

3. **I'm banned from the school.** It does happen, from time to time, that a parent becomes *persona non grata* on campus. All the more reason to go during regularly scheduled public entrance times. It's unlikely you'll be kicked out if you are participating in a public event. But—behave yourself, okay?

Keep In Mind

You may have informal opportunities to talk with the teacher if you pick your child up from school or volunteer in the school building. Those spontaneous meetings are great for fostering relationships and getting quick notice of praise or problems. But don't turn them into conferences with agendas. For serious conversations, you'll want to make sure you schedule some time just for the two of you. Ambush meetings aren't fair or helpful. Plus, the other parents waiting to pick up their kids will curse you.

10   Keep a Contact Log

You're talking to the teacher. You're writing notes. You're staying in touch. You're e-mailing. You're communicating like crazy. That's great.

Now, do you remember who you talked to about what when and what answers were given or what plans were made?

If you were keeping a contact log, you would.

If you were keeping a contact log, you could say, "Ms. Jones, as you'll recall, we spoke on March 26 about the problem with Joey bending the corners of his papers, and you agreed to consult with the occupational therapist about getting him a fidget toy to occupy his hands."

Instead of, "Hey, you remember, we talked about this that time, and you said you'd talk to that person about getting one of those things?"

Keeping a good record of communications—all communications, from informal notes to pick-up chats to formal meetings—puts you in a very powerful position. It means that you can always refer to exactly what was discussed and promised. And it means that educators know that you can always refer to exactly what was discussed and promised. Removing deniability from the conversation has a way of focusing everyone's attention.

This doesn't mean you should go sneaking around, whispering notes into a tape recorder hidden in your overcoat, stockpiling details for some big ambush. Be pleasantly up-front about keeping a log. Write letters after meetings to confirm conversations. When plans are made, ask what date you should check back, and let everybody see you jot that date down. Keep all that information in a notebook, a datebook, an online database, a PDA, whatever works for you and allows you to access the information easily.

You may find yourself becoming, essentially, the recording secretary for your child's IEP planning team, the person everyone can count on to have the details and the paper trail. Since you're focused exclusively on one case and they're juggling many, you'll probably have the clearest record of what's been talked about and strategized. Bring your contact log with you to meetings, for everybody's benefit. Hold on to the records from previous years as well—particularly if the personnel you're working with are shuffled around frequently. You may wind up being Team Historian as well as secretary.

And should you at some point have to dispute an IEP or file a complaint? You've got a handy listing of smoking guns to detail to the decision-makers on the case. With luck, the very fact that you have that, and everybody knows that you do, will keep things from getting that far.

Five Good Reasons to Do It

1. You have a good record of your child's school year.
2. It's easy to hold others accountable.
3. Since others know you can hold them accountable, they have incentive to be accountable.
4. You'll be a more valued member of the IEP team.
5. Anything that keeps you from having to rely on your poor frazzled memory is probably a good thing.

Three Bad Reasons Not To

1. **I'll remember what I need to.** Even if you could—and you probably can't, in sufficient detail—a written record will be more persuasive proof of conversations had and agreements made than your verbal description of what's in your brain. Jotting the date, time, and outcome of communications is simple enough to do that there's no reason to rely on remembering.

2. **I like to keep things off the record.** There's something to be said for having an informal, gossipy relationship with certain key school personnel, and yes, you may want to keep that on the down-low to keep all of you from incriminating yourselves. But do keep a log to record more formal contacts. When folks are on the record, record what they say.

3. **It will seem like a hostile gesture.** In the highly charged atmosphere of some school disputes, taking notes can seem like taking aim. But it doesn't have to. Does a secretary taking minutes at an organizational meeting seem like open hostility? Keeping track of facts, especially if you're doing it in a pleasant and transparent fashion, shouldn't raise anybody's hackles.

Keep In Mind

The information you keep in your contact log will vary with your needs, your patience, and your personality. However, there are some things you'll want to make sure are included:

- *Date (and time, if applicable) of contact*
- *Mode of contact (note, letter, e-mail, phone call, informal meeting, formal meeting, etc.)*
- *Name, function, and contact information of person contacted*
- *Purpose of the contact*
- *Outcome of the contact*
- *Follow-up needed, and who is responsible*

You may want to make up a form with each of these categories included, fill it out for each contact, and keep the pages in a three-ring binder.

11   Support the Teacher at Home

Hey. Just between us: You have an opinion about your child's teacher, don't you?

Maybe it's mostly good, except for that one thing she does that drives you crazy. Maybe you think he's too strict or too lenient. Maybe you could easily fill an hour ranting about how the teacher doesn't follow the IEP, doesn't honor the behavior plan, doesn't have a heart or a brain or a spine.

You're human. You have an opinion. But here's the thing: Keep it to yourself.

You may feel like you're supporting your child when you bad-talk the teacher in front of her. When he's struggling with homework, it seems natural to say "That teacher gives too much work!" When she's upset over a classroom slight, it seems right and good to assure your child that she's right and the teacher is wrong.

But more than likely, you're setting your child up for problems—problems that will hurt your student more than yourself, and hurt his school success most of all.

Kids are sponges for our words and our thoughts and our stress. They respect what we respect, and dis what we dis. Give a child permission, based on your own behavior, to disregard or dislike a teacher, and that may manifest in ways you would never have wished.

At the least, it may cause the teacher to dislike your child right back, and you as well, and work less zealously on your behalf. At worst, it may set up a behavioral struggle that puts your child at risk of school disruption. What it won't do, pretty much for sure, is make things better for anybody.

This is not to say you won't have to fight battles with teachers. There are always going to be conflicts. But keep it between the adults, and keep it at a mature level.

Free and open communication between you and the teacher and you and the school—all that note writing and meeting having and conferencing we've been talking about—will do a lot more to remedy unacceptable situations than ranting and raving at home without ever getting the side of the story of the person you're raging at or letting that person know yours.

Demonstrate basic respect for the teacher in front of your child and continue to do so in all those places where you think your child can't hear you but have found from sad experience that she can. Unless you want your words and attitudes echoed back in the classroom, causing trouble without you.

Five Good Reasons to Do It

1. Most teachers are hard-working, well-meaning individuals, even the ones you don't like or agree with.

2. You wouldn't want the teacher saying bad things about you in front of your child.

3. Being supportive can get you in good with the teacher, which may make whatever problem you're having go away on its own.

4. When you have a positive attitude, things tend to change for the positive.

5. When you have a negative attitude, things tend to change for the negative.

Three Bad Reasons Not To

1. **Supporting my child is the most important thing.** Sure it is. But being unsupportive of the teacher in front of your child is a bad way to support your child, if you can follow that. Supporting your child means creating the best possible environment at home and at school, and all that negativity does neither.

2. **That teacher is a jerk!** Glad you got that off your chest. But if you say that in front of your child, and your child says that in front of the class, there's going to be heck to

pay. Model maturity for your child and handle things through the proper channels.

3. **My child doesn't understand what I'm saying anyway.** Maybe not. But he probably understands stress and he probably picks up when you're angry. Even kids who spend most of their time in their own worlds know when our world is getting rocked and who's doing the rocking. Don't add that layer of stress and confusion onto an already difficult school day. These battles may be about your child, but they're not your child's to fight.

Keep In Mind

It's important to listen to your child. Absolutely. Children and the troubling things they report need to be taken seriously. But it's also important to realize that sometimes your child gets things wrong. Chances are, your child has said misleading things about you, and you've trusted that other adults would give you the benefit of the doubt and be open to your interpretation. Extend the same benefit to teachers when your child comes home with some outrageous and hurtful story. The truth may be less worth getting up-in-arms about than you think.

12 Support the Teacher in Public

There's a lot of talk about how "kids today" are rude, fresh, out-of-control behaviorally, and unwilling to take the direction of adults.

But you know what? I'm a lot more worried about the way some of those adults behave toward other adults.

Children have the excuse of being immature and of testing authority as a necessary part of growing up.

I don't know what the excuse is, though, for the parent I saw yell at a teacher at back-to-school night until she made that teacher cry. I don't know what the excuse is for the parent who argued outside a church-school classroom over whether her child had misbehaved sufficiently to be sent home, while the child stood smugly by soaking all that attitude in.

I'm sure those moms felt like powerful advocates, but the way it turned out, they were just bullies.

This is not to say that you should never speak up when you disagree with a teacher's decision, and it's true that oftentimes grand gestures get more attention than going through proper channels. But in the long run, bullying parents lead directly to timid administrators and restrictive policies, and a lack of flexibility that often swings around to harm children with special behavioral and disciplinary needs most of all.

It also can get you banned from school property pretty quick, preventing you from being exactly the sort of proactive parent you thought you were being.

Often, teachers are in the awkward position of being the public face of administrative decisions. They're the ones who have to enforce rules and put plans in place. Getting unpopular policies changed can be a great way of supporting your child's teacher and education, but you can't do it if you never get past killing the messenger. Communication—civil, if it can't be friendly—is the key to getting that information and applying your advocacy in the most responsible and effective way.

You and your child's teacher can be each other's greatest allies. If the teacher feels you're supportive, you may hear things you wouldn't have otherwise, and learn more about what's needed. You'll have more opportunities to help and promote and be a positive force instead of a negative one.

You'd like to think that the teacher would support you in front of others, and support parents in general as an important part of their children's lives, right? Return the favor.

Five Good Reasons to Do It

1. Most teachers are hard-working, well-meaning individuals, even the ones you don't like or agree with.

2. Being publicly unsupportive is a good way to get branded as a troublemaker.

3. And being publicly supportive can get you branded as someone to trust.

4. Your child may pick up your aggressive attitude and get in trouble.

5. You'd want the teacher to be supportive of you.

Three Bad Reasons Not To

1. **People only listen when you're in their face.** It certainly seems like that sometimes, doesn't it? But how do you feel about the coworker or acquaintance or family member who follows that policy with you? Are you inclined to go out of your way to help that person? You may win the battle but lose a very important war.

2. **I'm just one of a group of parents who are all speaking out.** And if that group of parents was jumping off a bridge, would you jump, too? Ganging up on somebody is no better a way to solve a problem now than it was when you were kids in the schoolyard. Group advocacy can sometimes be useful, but not if it's a lynch mob.

3. **The teacher works for me.** Technically, if you're a tax- or tuition-payer, that's so. But the teacher also works for a school district that may have very different ideas of how to

do things than you do. And most importantly, the teacher works for your child, and that's the relationship you want to preserve. Your lack of support reflects on your child and is reflected by your child.

Keep In Mind

We've been talking a lot about handling teachers you disagree with, and funneling that disagreement through the proper channels. But maybe you like your child's teacher. Love her! Think he's great! It's easy to be supportive then, isn't it? How supportive are you really, though? Have you ever written a letter to the teacher's superiors offering praise for the work the teacher does? Have you ever asked whether the teacher could use some help, either in the classroom or with supplies? Do you speak well of the teacher when you're talking with special-education personnel, or other parents? A little gratitude goes a long way with people who are too often in a thankless job. Let your support show.

13   Address Problems Promptly and Positively

One school year, I heard that my son was having a problem in class. He was slipping his shoes off, which caused his one-on-one aide to prompt him verbally to put them back on. This was repeated over and over again throughout the day—I think a behavior specialist counted thirty times in one hour—creating a stressful situation for him, the aide, and no doubt for the rest of the class as well.

Unfortunately, the school year I heard about this happening was not the school year in which it actually occurred. It was at the beginning of the next school year, by which time it was far too late to do anything about it.

And there was plenty I could have done. I could have sent him to school in lace-up work boots that would have been difficult to slip off. I could have asked the occupational therapist to put a band around his chair for his feet to fidget with. I could have suggested some other methods for the aide to try, such as a reward for not slipping the shoes off. Or I could have worked with the teacher on a behavior plan under which shoe-slipping wasn't a big deal (as indeed, it wasn't for the teacher that following year).

For whatever reason, the teacher and the aide did not think it was necessary to trouble me with this particular classroom issue, and as a result, a small problem became a big one. Don't do the same when you see a problem with your child's class work or classroom experience. Bring problems up when they're still small. Maybe they can be solved easily and maybe they can't, but at least they'll be out in the open.

We've talked about being supportive of the teacher, and it may seem like one way to do that is not to complain about little things. But pointing out problems isn't the same as complaining about them. And nipping difficult situations in the bud—in a positive way—is entirely supportive of both your teacher and your struggling child.

It's all in the way the matter is approached. What I would have liked is for the teacher to have said to me, "I notice that your son slips his shoes off a lot. It's distracting to him and to the class, and I wonder if you have any ideas about that would help with that." Not, "Teach your kid to keep his *#%& shoes on!" but a call for collaboration among parties who care for him.

You can do the same. Approach problems as a mutual dilemma. Ask to work things out together in a way that is mutually satisfactory. You're supposed to be a team. So team up to make problems go away before they become insurmountable.

Five Good Reasons to Do It
1. Small problems are easier to fix than big ones.
2. You look like an involved and interested parent.

3. The teacher may have ideas for problems you're having at home, too.

4. The teacher will be more likely to come to you for future problems, rather than forwarding them to the administration.

5. It's easier to negotiate with the teacher now than the IEP team later.

Three Bad Reasons Not To

1. **I don't want to be a whiner.** So don't be. Be a problem-solver. If you're approaching things in a positive and collaborative way, you're being supportive.

2. **I like to focus on the good things, not the problems.** As well you should! But resolving issues quickly is a good thing and causes more good things to occur. Problems ignored become problems that are impossible to ignore, and then it will be hard to find any good things to focus on at all.

3. **The teacher denies that there are any problems.** Sometimes teachers want to handle everything themselves, and there's not much you can do about that . . . except enter the fact that you tried to discuss it in your contact log, list the suggestions you made, and be ready to document that, should the problem spring up again in a meeting.

Keep In Mind

The word "problem" here may be a problem, since it implies something negative and troubling. If it seems like your child has no problems, that's great—but broaden your thinking a little bit. Is there something that's fine, but could be better? You don't need to make mountains out of molehills, but if something's bugging you or just doesn't seem right, think of how you could approach it in a positive, collaborative, problem-solving way. Then ask the teacher if she considers this issue to be a problem, and mention that if it does become a problem, here's how you would suggest handling it.

14   Make Sure the Assignments Make It Home

Before you can help with homework and supervise homework and support homework, the homework has to come home in the first place.

The standard assumption when a child doesn't bring assignments home is that he is purposely ducking work. Sometimes, that may be so (and admit it, when your child comes home saying "No homework," you're sometimes so secretly relieved that you don't want to ask too many questions).

But sometimes, the very disabilities these students are in special education for in the first place—poor reading and writing skills; visual or auditory perception problems; executive function problems that impair the ability to organize or schedule; distractibility—have a direct impact on their ability to get it together to carry that assignment info home.

Not helping is the fact that many of the pull-outs they get to service those special needs—for resource room or speech or occupational therapy or physical therapy—make it easy to miss homework details and handouts.

Like homework delivery, this is an issue that is going to require some close collaboration between you and the teacher. Start by asking how the assignment information is given out:

▶ If it's written on the board, is your child sitting where she can see it? Is the information always written in the same place? Is it clearly visible or lost in the day's lessons and notes? Are students specifically told to copy the information?

▶ Is the information given out orally, with students expected to write it down? Is a clear prompt given to let everyone know to write the information down? Is there a written version somewhere to double-check? What if a student is out of the classroom at the time?

▶ If assignment information is placed in a folder for students to check, are they prompted to do that or expected to remember on their own? Do students who leave early or arrive late have an opportunity to check?

After discussion with the teacher, you may be able to identify some of the reasons your child is not able to successfully jot down assignments. Sometimes the solution is as simple as making sure your student has an assignment pad on which to note homework, and asking the teacher or aide to check it at the end of the day to confirm that it's complete. Sometimes you may want to request that a homework sheet be given to your child; you can check off the items as your child completes them, and send the sheet back to help with delivery.

E-mail and school websites with assignments listed are other good ways to bypass your child's poor reporting skills and get the word directly from the source. And if all else fails, exchange numbers with the parents of another child in the class, and check among yourselves to figure out what that assignment was supposed to be. Maybe between two kids, you'll get one complete list.

Five Good Reasons to Do It

1. It's appropriate for your child to get accommodations in this area if needed.
2. Homework is too important to let this go untried.
3. Organizational tricks learned now will benefit your child throughout school.
4. Arrangements worked out now can make good IEP provisions later.
5. You'll get a good sense of how things work in the classroom by conferring with the teacher about this. (Maybe he's disorganized, too.)

Three Bad Reasons Not To

1. **My child has to learn how to do this for herself.** And she's going to learn it . . . how? Use this as an opportunity to teach her how to overcome her natural lack of organizational skills. A lightning bolt's not going to come and hit her with it.

2. **It's the teacher's responsibility to make sure kids have the assignments.** In a perfect world, every teacher would be completely tuned in to the unique needs of every student. But as it usually happens, if most kids are bringing home the homework, the teacher's going to assume there's no problem. Do everybody a favor and point it out.

3. **The teacher won't cooperate with this.** If it's in your child's IEP, the teacher doesn't really have a choice (though he'll probably farm it out to a paraprofessional). You'll hope to come to a friendly agreement about it, but should your concerns go unheard, take them to your case manager.

Keep In Mind

Most folks acknowledge that kids can have problems with words or numbers, writing or reading, composition or comprehension. Why do we all expect organizational skills to come naturally? Like everything else, they're easy for some kids and hard for others. Struggles with organization do not mean laziness or sloppiness, just a different brain pattern. Accommodate it like anything else.

15   Learn to Love Homework

Hate homework? Think your child has too much of it? Join the club. Plenty of parents of children in regular education have protested the homework load. If your child has trouble reading, writing, learning, or staying in one place for very long, that burden may fall all the more heavily on you.

But as hard as homework may be for kids in special education, it may also be most important for them. Reinforcement and repetition are essential tools for struggling learners. Practice away from the classroom ensures that material has really been learned. Reluctant writers and readers need encouragement and enrichment at home, and homework is a convenient way to provide it.

Next time you're tempted to say, "But my child has special needs. My child needs special treatment. My child works so hard during the day. My child needs a break," think of this: Your child misses out on many, many normal childhood experiences because of her special needs. Homework is something that all kids do; it's a normal school thing. Don't deprive your child of the experience of doing homework—and if you must, be sure it's really because your *child* can't tolerate it, and not because *you* can't.

Aside from the academic benefits of homework and the just-a-regular-kid benefits, there's one more benefit that you'll never hear about at school. It's a whopper, though: Homework gives you the ability to spy on your child's teacher.

You may not be able to spend time in your child's classroom. But you can see what's going on in it by watching the work that comes home. Does it seem hard enough to you? Does it seem too hard? Is there a noticeable progression of skill as the months go by? What grade level are the workbooks that your child brings home? Look up the titles on the Internet, and you may find some interesting facts.

Compare the worksheets that are being done for homework to the items on your child's IEP, if you can bear to look at that scary document. Does it seem consistent with your child's goals? Look for other evidence of progress. If your child is supposed to be working on writing in therapy, is his writing getting neater?

If your child never handles a sum or writes a letter at home, how are you going to know what she can do? You will be at the mercy of professionals telling you your child can or cannot do something, and that's not a good place to be. Trust, but verify.

There's one more great advantage to having your child do homework faithfully: A whole lot of kids don't. Teachers have to feel discouraged when they give out assignments only to have them ignored by a large percentage of students. Your child's cooperation will reflect well on him and on your family, and sometimes it doesn't take much more than that to get into a teacher's good graces.

Most teachers also give points for homework completion, and those can go a long way toward offsetting any bad scores your child makes on in-class quizzes and tests. Good homework habits have landed my daughter on the honor roll before. Why would you want to throw that advantage away?

Five Good Reasons to Do It

1. You can track your child's academic progress.
2. You show your child that you take school seriously.
3. You show the teacher that you take school seriously.
4. You discover more about how your child learns.
5. Your child earns points to offset poor test scores.

Three Bad Reasons Not To

1. **It's too hard.** Is that a message you want to give your child—it's too hard, baby, you don't have to do it? Adjust the workload with the teacher if necessary, but your child will benefit from meeting reasonable demands.
2. **There's no time.** The combination of increased time needed for homework and increased time needed for doctor and therapy appointments can create a homework time-crunch. Let the teacher know what days are problems, and see if your child can make up the work on less-scheduled nights or weekends.

3. **My child works all day, and needs a rest.** There should be time for work and still be time for rest. Teaching your child how to make productive use of time can be a great side-benefit of homework.

Keep in Mind

When approaching a teacher regarding a change in homework amount or timing, be very sure to assert that you want your child to do homework, you feel the work is important, and you want to find a way to make it happen. Going in with excuses and defensiveness will make the teacher defensive too, and no good is going to come of that.

16   Help with Homework, but Don't Do All the Work

Here's your homework: Don't do homework.

You will, absolutely, want to help with homework. Supervise homework. Police homework. Strategize homework. Check homework.

Do everything about homework except *do* the homework.

That's easier said than done, I know. Most parents are not trained educators. We haven't been to school to learn how to draw information out of a child without handing it over. Particularly when children have disabilities, parents get used to doing things for them, and working to prevent frustration. When your child doesn't get something, and you can't figure out how to teach it, it's tempting to just say, "Say this."

But there are a couple of problems with that.

For one, the teacher doesn't want to know if you get it, the teacher wants to know if your child gets it.

For another, the degree to which your child doesn't get it and the ways in which it is not gotten can be useful information to a teacher.

Still, it can be hard when your child needs help—help you're not trained to give in a useful way and help he's not able to receive with complete independence. How many times do you try to explain how your child can find the answer before you just dictate it to her?

Resist the urge. Let your child get it wrong or leave it blank. Write a note to the teacher explaining that your child struggled with the work. And if it's too distressing for your child or yourself not to complete it, write a note to the teacher explaining that the work was done with a high degree of parental input.

Your child may sometimes receive assignments that seem impossible to do without significant assistance—a big report or project, perhaps. That's a good excuse to call or e-mail the teacher and ask for some advice on how to handle it. What degree of participation from you will be acceptable? If the amount the teacher suggests is less than you think your child needs, share that concern and ask for some input on how the teacher expects your student to do that.

A resolution not to *do* the homework doesn't mean you can't *look* at the homework. In looking work over, you may see that your child is making an obvious mistake you can help him address or she is copying words from the book or the Internet in a way that could cause trouble. Talking problems and subjects over doesn't cross the line of doing homework, but if you have any doubt, drop a line to the teacher. That should help establish a balance between keeping the school informed and keeping your child from getting too frustrated.

Five Good Reasons to Do It

1. You already graduated from school, right? You're not the one who needs to study.

2. The teacher can tell when the work is yours.

3. The goal of homework is practice, not perfection.

4. You don't want to make your child more dependent.

5. If you haven't been in class for the lesson, there's a good chance you might get the answers wrong.

Three Bad Reasons Not To

1. **He'll get a bad grade if I don't.** Maybe not. Teachers often give credit for homework completed, regardless of correctness. Check with the teacher to see if, indeed, effort is what counts. If not, that may be something to add to your child's IEP.

2. **My child can't do it without me.** If that's really true, then the homework's too hard. Talk to the teacher about that. More likely, though, your child can do it but would rather have you do it instead. You may have to survive some whining, but it's worth it to give your child an experience of standing on her own.

3. **There's not enough time for my child to do it all.** And if that's really true, then there's too much homework. Talk to the teacher about *that*. The last thing you want to do is

convince your child that if it takes too long, you'll do it. Because then he knows to work s-l-o-w.

Keep In Mind

Have you ever had the experience of receiving an art project allegedly done by your child at school that was clearly created by an adult? The coloring's a little too inside the lines, the cutting's a little too exact, the composition's a little too balanced. It's a lovely piece of artwork, and yet . . . you'd rather see your child's smears and lumps and gashes than this obvious imposter. Think about that next time you help with homework. The teacher doesn't want to see your perfect A+ artwork. Don't take the project over. Let the smears and lumps and gashes show. The teacher will know the difference, too.

17   Make Sure the Homework Gets Delivered

A funny thing happens on the way to the classroom: Homework that was done disappears. Into the bottom of the book bag, into the back of the locker, into thin air! Since credit for work done is only due when that work is turned in, a lot of homework time can be wasted with nothing to show for it.

When that happens, it's easy to blame the nonmessenger, and tell your student that the responsibility for delivery is all on him. Trouble is, if your child has special needs that impair organization, all the will and desire in the world is not going to get that homework where it's going. You've acknowledged that your child needs special assistance with things like reading and writing and math. Acknowledge that special assistance may be needed in paper management, too.

One thing you can do to support that, right at home, is make a visual confirmation that the homework has hit the book bag. Watch your child put her homework in her book bag, and look again before the book bag goes on the back at school time. It may help to have a special folder just for assignments to be returned. If desperate measures are called for, a clear backpack can make checking contents even easier. However you do it, you want to make sure that when your child leaves for school, those hard-worked-on assignments leave with her.

Of course, getting the paperwork to *school* is only one-half of the challenge. Getting it to the *teacher* is the other. And that's going to take some teamwork.

If chronic nondelivery of homework is a problem, that's a good reason to have a meeting with the teacher. See if you can establish a system that makes it easier for your child to fulfill his responsibility to turn homework in. Again, a special folder for homework may help, but the teacher will need to ask for it instead of expecting your child to hand it over. If your child changes classes and forgets assignments in his locker, try a super-large binder in which he can tote the material for all classes and keep it close at hand.

Since it's hard for you to know whether homework is delivered or not, send a checklist in that the teacher can mark when work is received. You can also mark that work has been done, so that the teacher knows to ask for it. Of course, if your child can't keep track of work, he probably can't keep track of a checklist, either. You did get that teacher's e-mail address, right?

Five Good Reasons to Do It

1. All that homework work should be good for something.
2. Your child shouldn't get in trouble for not doing something she really did.
3. Increased collaboration between home and school reaps all sorts of benefits.

4. Arrangements you work out now can make good IEP provisions later.

5. Organizational skills are always going to be a challenge, so it's good to work up some compensating techniques while the stakes are small.

Three Bad Reasons Not To

1. **I'm trying to teach my child responsibility here.** Terrific. But teaching involves providing instruction and example before expecting a student to perform a skill independently. Don't assume your child knows how to be organized just because you do.

2. **I have no way of knowing where the homework goes when it gets to school.** No, but you have a way of knowing how it gets there, and whether that's neatly in a folder or crumpled at the bottom of a book bag. Go through your child's bag, and you may be surprised to find how many things are tucked hither and yon between pages of books or folded into tiny squares in corners of folders. That stuff you can fix, and you should.

3. **I'm disorganized, too.** Then what you have here is a family project. Set a homework-delivery goal for your child, an organizational goal for yourself, and chart your progress

together. Doing something better than a parent is pretty fine motivation for a kid.

Keep In Mind

When talking to a teacher about homework delivery, make it clear that you don't want to absolve your child of the responsibility, so much as make the responsibility appropriate to your child's abilities. Just as you wouldn't expect a student at a second-grade level in math to do advanced algebra, it's unrealistic to expect a child with underdeveloped organizational skills to keep track of papers without assistance. Start out by thinking about the ways you would handle homework delivery with a much younger child, and set some goals to bringing your student along to a more mature handling of the work. If necessary, have these arrangements formalized as part of the IEP.

18   Share What Works and What Doesn't

Besides giving your child needed practice on schoolwork and the teacher needed information about just how much your child gets it or doesn't, homework is also good for giving *you* a clue. Unless you work directly with your child, learning challenges can be pretty abstract. You may nod your head blankly when the therapist talks about low muscle tone or poor motor planning, but when you have to watch your child loosely grip a pencil and wave it all over a poor piece of paper while trying to write, you start to see what that means.

If you're like most parents of children with special needs, when you see your child struggling, you set about finding a way to make things easier. That's another reason why it's important for you to take the homework seriously, because otherwise that struggle will only be seen by teachers and aides. When it's happening at your kitchen table, punctuated by shouting and slamming and tears, it puts you on the job in a way notes home from the teacher really don't.

So consult with other parents to see how they've handled the problem. Do some research on remedies. Buy some pencil grips or high-lined paper; make flashcards or cardboard windows to isolate math problems; record reading material or make up mnemonics.

Experiment around and see what's effective for getting your child's brain working and the results on paper.

Then, share what you've found with your child's teacher.

It should be part of the collaborative process that you're developing with all these notes and phone calls and meetings that you share successes and puzzle together over problems. Ask the teacher to let you know what's working inside the classroom, and return the favor by suggesting tips and tricks that have made work easier at home. Consistency between the approaches used in those two environments will help your child, too.

Of course, when the things you try *don't* work, or you can't seem to find a way to help your child with a particular challenge, those are issues to bring to the teacher as well. School personnel need to know when your child has a horrible time with something that's homework. They may have a solution to offer you, or it may be time to back off and try something else for a while.

It's a give and take, or should be. You'll know you've established a good record of thinking up solutions that help your child be successful when the teacher starts coming to *you* for suggestions.

Five Good Reasons to Do It

1. Everyone working with your child should be on the same page.
2. The more minds working on solutions, the better.

3. Thanks to parent support groups, you may have access to information and ideas that teachers don't.

4. You've spent a lifetime figuring out what works for your child. The teacher has nine months.

5. Might as well get maximum benefit out of that miserable homework.

Three Bad Reasons Not To

1. **I'm not a professional**—the teacher won't be interested in what I have to say. As long as you're an expert on your child, you have a place in recommending strategies for learning. If the teacher chooses not to listen, there's nothing you can do about it, but you've got to give it a try. Next year, perhaps, you'll get a more amenable teacher who you can share your ideas with.

2. **I don't have time to do all this research.** Really? Because it probably takes less time than all the fighting you're doing when your child gets caught up in fussing and frustration. The Internet has made it easy to seek information and friendly advice. Make this *your* homework.

3. **The teacher's paid to tell me what works and what doesn't.** And that should happen, absolutely. It's a teacher's job to do that. But it's *your* job as a parent to work hard to make things better in all areas of your child's life. Just as

you might try some home remedies and share the information with the doctor, do your job at the homework table and share your thoughts with the teacher. Your pay comes in the form of your child's success.

Keep In Mind

Here's how you can tell the difference between a bad teacher, a good teacher, and a great teacher: When you share some strategies that have worked with your child at home, a bad teacher will get all territorial and make it clear that your unprofessional suggestions are not wanted. A good teacher will receive your suggestions and attempt to implement them. A great teacher will implement them, then come back to you with ways to improve them. What kind of teacher does your child have? Offer some advice and see.

19   Keep a Record of What Your Child Is Working On

Do you keep your child's old school papers around? Me too. And maybe like yours, mine tend to pile up over the course of marking periods and school years until I finally tackle that unmanageable stack and do some sorting.

I remember one year, when I was sorting two school years' worth of papers, I noticed a discomfiting thing: The work my son had done the second year was more or less identical to the work he had done the first. Turns out, the second-year teacher had been misinformed about his progress and had him working at a lower level than he should have been.

Oops.

If I'd been really keeping track of his homework and what skills he was working on, rather than just taking things day by day, I'd have noticed, and he'd have made more progress academically that year.

One good thing to do, obviously, is to review those stacks of papers when they come back home and keep the body of work your child is producing fresh in your mind. Another is to keep a list for each subject and jot down the skills your child is working on. The IEP can be a guide here, but often those goals are only part of what gets covered if the teacher follows a particular grade-level's curriculum.

Should you find that your child is spending a lot of homework time on something that has been previously mastered, that's a good prompt to have a conversation with the teacher. It may be that your child needs a review, or that the teacher's method is to go over something, take a break from it, then go over it again to make sure your child really owns the skill. The beginning of each school year, too, is usually a time for going back over what's already been done.

It may be, though, that there's been some administrative error, or some wrong homework given. If you can be the one to point this out pleasantly, you'll help your student and her teacher both. Bring those old papers along to illustrate and approach the issue in a friendly, collaborative way. You may find out something about how your child learns or help your child learn something new. Finally.

Five Good Reasons to Do It

1. It's a good way to monitor your child's progress or lack thereof.
2. You'll be able to make a meaningful contribution to the discussion of goals at IEP meetings.

3. Even good teachers sometimes get bad information.
4. If you need to use tutors or summertime help, you'll be able to show exactly where your child is at.
5. Maybe all that clutter won't build up quite so high.

Three Bad Reasons Not To

1. **It's the teacher's job to keep track of these things.** It's also the teacher's job to keep track of grades and attendance, but if you saw something wrong there, you'd speak up. Think of yourself as the backup plan.

2. **I don't know what level my child's homework is at.** You don't need to. Just jot down the skills being worked on—often, they're mentioned at the top of the page. Two-digit addition. Noun-verb agreement. That sort of thing. The more basic you make it, the more likely you'll be able to spot overlaps.

3. **All my child's teacher ever sends home is meaningless busy work.** That's certainly something to have a parent-teacher conversation about, since homework should bear some relation to what's being done in class or what is its purpose? (Seriously, ask the teacher: "What is its purpose?" There may be one.) A record of what's been sent home is a good basis on which to start that chat.

Keep In Mind

When those big bundles of expired papers come home at the end of a marking period, it's often hard to remember which pieces were homework and which ones were in-class work. But that's useful information, because if the homework doesn't match up with what you now see your child was working on in class, that teacher has some explaining to do. If you've kept a homework record, you can keep track of papers that are on different subjects than you've noted down. If that's too much work, though, you can also put a light "X" mark in a corner on the back of your child's homework assignments, something that won't be noticeable unless you're looking for it, as you will be later. Sort those papers into homework and class work, compare the two, and bring the evidence along if you see discrepancies you need to discuss. Proof is lots more effective than, "Well, it just sort of kind of seems like this isn't what I remember we were working on three months ago."

20   Volunteer in the Classroom

You can spy on your child's classroom via the homework he does and the classroom papers she brings home. You can get an impression of the teacher and the classroom by scheduling regular conferences. But you'll never get close to knowing what your child goes through each and every school day without actually viewing a class in progress.

Of course, that doesn't mean you're necessarily going to like what you see.

Observing the class in progress means noticing that your child doesn't seem to interact with other students or that other students treat him roughly. It means watching your child act up in disruptive ways or sit motionless and zoned out. It means understanding that your child struggles with work more than the others or is so far ahead of the others in terms of academic ability that he's bored, or underserved by overwhelmed teachers.

None of those things are comfortable for a parent to watch. All of those are important for a parent to know.

While you might hear from official sources that your child is disruptive, nobody's going to tell you if there's another disruptive child who hijacks the class and upsets your kid. Nobody's going to tell you about the noise coming in from the parking lot that distracts your child or the flickering light or the fact that the one kid in class your child can't stand is always grouped with her for projects.

You're never going to get to be in a classroom long enough to know all that goes on. But you can be there long enough to pick up on some of the human dynamics—between the kids in the classroom, the kids and the adults, and the adults among themselves. Workplace issues between aides and teachers in a classroom can set a tense tone that sets kids off, too.

So how do you get into the classroom? Snap up any opportunities that arise. If class parents get to throw parties on holidays, volunteer for that. If they seek parent volunteers to read stories, pick a book. If there's a Grandparent or Special Person day, send a relative or friend in with some ideas on what to look for. Some schools actively seek parent participation and others don't, but let the teacher know you're available either way.

And if you want to be invited back, don't use the information you gain as a blunt instrument to force the school to make changes. That's a pretty good way to make sure you never see the inside of a classroom again. Your time in school should give you compassion for the people who work there and go to school there and a desire to make suggestions for improvement. If you can spearhead some of those suggestions yourself, all the better.

Being in the classroom should also give you some new ideas of what to ask about when your child comes home from school. You'll know what to ask if you've been there.

Five Good Reasons to Do It

1. It lets your child know you're interested in what he does all day.
2. It lets the teacher know you're willing and available to provide support.
3. You'll get a close-up look at any trouble spots.
4. You may spot a child or two who looks like a good prospect for play dates.
5. It will inform your interaction with your child and the teacher.

Three Bad Reasons Not To

1. **I work during the day.** Try hard to get the time off if an opportunity to volunteer arises. You don't have to do it often—maybe once a marking period or so—but don't make your child be that only student in the class who never gets to show off a parent.
2. **The school doesn't want me there.** That'll happen, particularly if you're perceived as a troublemaker. But there will often be classroom opportunities open to all parents that

will be hard to keep you out of. Look out for those Special Person days and story-reading days and other days in which classrooms are opened up, and take *responsible* advantage of them.

3. **My child doesn't want me there.** Some kids have a very hard time seeing somebody from the Home Realm suddenly turn up in the School Realm. They'd really rather not have worlds collide. Be sensitive to that. But do it anyway.

Keep In Mind

Sometimes it's not so much a case of your child not wanting you there as your child not being able to behave when you are. If your presence in the classroom causes such over-the-top behavior from your child that it disrupts any semblance of normal class, then you're probably better off volunteering in the school rather than the classroom. But make sure to do that.

21 Volunteer in the School

Some schools make parent volunteering a prerequisite of attendance. Some encourage it and benefit greatly from the enrichment activities parents provide. Some have a few specific jobs parents are allowed to do under certain limitations. And others really don't want to see you between drop-off and pick-up time at all.

If your school is in that latter group, it looks like you're off the hook. But if the school allows *any* sort of parent involvement, find a way to be one of those involved parents.

Volunteering in the classroom is only one facet of this. Doing other volunteer work around the school—in the library, in the lunchroom, on the playground, doing book sales or club activities or event planning—can bring benefits beyond those that a classroom visitation can offer.

For one thing, you get the good gossip.

Being present in school hallways and public rooms makes you available for casual conversations with teachers and other school personnel. Build up friendly relationships, and you may hear things informally that you'd never get in a conference setting. People who work in schools are just like people who work anyplace else—they get frustrated, and they need to blow off steam. Being there when the top pops off can get you some excellent intelligence.

All the more so if you're willing to eavesdrop on conversations going on around you. Work diligently and frequently behind the scenes of your children's school for long enough, and you may blend into the woodwork sufficiently that school personnel won't think twice about chatting with each other in front of you. Go about your business, but keep your ears open. You may find out which teacher is least liked, which administrator is least capable, which student is most griped about, which policy is most hated.

And sometimes you don't have to listen very hard, because people will be yelling. Being a presence in your child's school is a great way to figure out which teachers scream at their students in the hallways, which teachers can't keep their students from screaming in the hallways, and which teachers you want to make sure your child is never exposed to. Other parents may learn that sort of thing through the neighborhood grapevine, but parents of children in special education are often not privy to that parental chitchat. Volunteering gives you a chance to get it firsthand.

School is where your child spends a high percentage of her life. Shouldn't you be a part of that place, too?

Five Good Reasons to Do It

1. It lets your child know that you're interested in what he does all day.

2. It lets school personnel know you're willing and available to provide support.

3. You'll get a close-up look at any trouble spots or troublesome people.

4. You'll be available for informal interactions with teachers and administrators.

5. Your good reputation as a helpful parent can rub off on your child.

Three Bad Reasons Not To

1. **I'm not available during the day.** Maybe not every day, or even very many days, but if there's a possibility at all that you may be able to schedule a day every so often, do so. Skip a lunch hour or take a half-day off or get a babysitter so you can support your child and be true to her school.

2. **I don't have a way to get to the school.** If your child is attending a school far from your neighborhood and you don't have wheels, that can indeed be a challenge. See if you can team up with another parent to get some transportation, ask a family member to give you a lift, or, if all else fails, call a cab.

3. **I never get information home about volunteer opportunities.** Yet most likely they exist. Call the school office and ask. Call the head of the parent organization. Better still, go

to a meeting (we'll get to that in the next chapter). Seek and most likely you'll find. At least let them know you're not getting papers from the school.

Keep In Mind

You may or may not have an opportunity to specifically view your child during these school volunteer opportunities. Library duty, for example, might involve checking out books to your child's class or to any class but. Similarly, your lunchroom or recess time can include your child's pals or exclude them. Often, the school makes the decision about whether parents can serve their own kids' class. If not, think about how important it is for you to see your child and be seen. We all like looking in on our precious offspring, but foregoing the opportunity to freak out your child with your presence may make for a less stressful volunteer experience for all concerned.

22   Go to Parent Organization Meetings

Oh, no! Anything but that!

If you're like me, that's your reaction to the suggestion that you should take a night out each month to go sit in a room and listen to grownups bicker about school politics. At best, it sounds like a pretty boring way to spend an evening. At worst, it will remind you of everything you hated about high school. Either way, you'll be pretty sure the time could have been better spent staying at home with your child.

Nevertheless, you need to go.

Once a month, you need to sit in a room with those people and hear what they have to say. You have to see and be seen. With parent organizations dwindling these days as fewer and fewer moms and dads make the effort, it's easier to be seen and recognized than ever.

And why should you want that?

Being a part of your school's parent organization gives you a chance to interact with other parents as a peer—not as someone on the wrong side of the educational tracks, but as a fellow concerned grownup ready to roll up your sleeves and help. It lets you get to know administrators in a nonadversarial context, so that when your child has a brush with trouble, he won't be just some kid but the child of someone who supports the school.

It doesn't mean your child or family will automatically get a pass, but every little bit helps.

At meetings, you'll also be first to know about volunteer opportunities that are available, or you can propose activities that might appeal to you or your child. You'll also hear a lot about the things regular-education students are getting involved in, and if you see special-education students being left out, speak up.

Best of all, your presence—and the presence of other parents like you, if you can scare up a few—can raise the visibility of children with special needs in the school. Chances are, if you've spent much time among parents involved in school activities, you've heard some crack or other about parents of kids in special education never showing up for anything.

You'll be on hand to say: Not so. We're here. And we're watching out for our kids.

Five Good Reasons to Do It

1. It introduces you to the players that keep the school humming.
2. It helps you get to know school personnel in a nonadversarial context.
3. It keeps you in-the-know on activities and volunteer opportunities.

4. You'll have a better idea of where special-education students are being slighted.

5. Hey, you could use an excuse to get out of the house, right?

Three Bad Reasons Not To

1. **I can't stand those people.** Aw, and they probably can't stand you. But you're not going for the witty repartee and good times; you're going to support your child and her school. And to make sure those people you can't stand don't ruin everything.

2. **It's too much of a time commitment.** Assuming you're just going to be a table-sitter and not a mover-and-shaker, it's an hour or two a month. Sure, you can get sucked into bigger commitments and some of that volunteer work you want. If you're pressed to do more, use the needs of your special child as an excuse. You're needed at home, you know? You can use that excuse to sneak out of meetings before they grind on to the end, too.

3. **I'm too involved with my other kids' school.** It's hard, for sure, when your child's special-education program places him at a different school than the one his siblings attend. But your participation and involvement in that school is as important as your participation and involvement in your neighborhood school. Think about how you feel about the

parents at the school you're involved in who never show up and never show an interest. Not kindly, most likely. Don't be one of those people at the other school just because your child's in special education. You don't have to be *as* involved, but c'mon. Make an appearance.

Keep In Mind

Parents who involve themselves in the school organization are excellent advocates not only for their children but for their children's teachers, making sure that supplies and trips and special projects get strong consideration. Special-education teachers often lack that voice in the greater school environment, and they and their students can suffer for it. You can raise that low profile by getting involved, and by letting teachers know you're willing to share their concerns at parent organization meetings. Anything you can do to keep kids like yours from being invisible and overlooked is worth doing, right? Even if there are a thousand things you'd rather be up to.

23 Help Your Child Join a Club

If your child's school has clubs and organizations and choirs and bands and teams of all types, you're likely to hear about how important it is for kids to get involved in the life of their school beyond simple academics. You'll hear how the best kids are the ones who have lots going on, and you'll want that for your child, too.

Then you'll ask how your child will be accommodated in all these wonderful activities, and you'll hear a lot of nothing.

Your child's IEP probably specifies that she should be included as much as appropriate in extracurricular activities, but when it gets down to the realities of a second round of bus pick-ups and additional hours for teachers or paraprofessionals, the plan starts to fall apart.

So put it back together.

Despite what you may be told, your child has every right to be a part of school organizations. Maybe the school doesn't "do that," but it can start. You may have to put some polite advocacy into it, but your child will benefit from being with other students in an environment apart from the classroom.

Ask your child's teacher to find out if there are any school clubs that would be open to including your child, and whether there's a teacher or aide who would be able to stay and help supervise. Find out which club-leading teachers might be most receptive to children with special needs and consider hooking up with their clubs.

If your child has musical ability, make sure he's considered for music lessons, chorus, band, orchestra, or whatever tuneful opportunities your school offers. Find out what's available, then figure out how you can make it happen. Be willing to provide transportation for early-morning or after-school rehearsals, and (maybe hardest of all) ensure that your child practices as promised.

It may seem like a lot of bother, especially if you have to provide transportation for your child and maybe others from her class who participate. But all those speeches you hear from educators are right—being part of the life of your school is an important part of being a student. It's important for your student, too; it just takes a little more support and effort and a parent with a big mouth.

Five Good Reasons to Do It

1. Your child will get the benefits of inclusion whether he's mainstreamed for class or not.
2. Being in clubs raises the profile of sometimes invisible special kids on campus.
3. Organizations strengthen friendships between classified and unclassified kids or between classified kids who club together.

4. You'll get to know some other families if you're dropping their kids off.

5. It's your child's right to do it. And isn't that what parents suit up for?

Three Bad Reasons Not To

1. **I was never in clubs in school.** And I suppose that worked for you. But you probably had lots more social opportunities outside of school than your special-needs child does. School organizations give your child something special to do in the place where she spends most of her time and has people who know and appreciate her. Don't dismiss that because it wasn't your thing back in the day.

2. **My child isn't interested in anything.** If there's nothing going on at your child's school that he wants to join . . . how about suggesting something new? The school may or may not bite, but it's worth a try. And if not, perhaps you can get some parents from your child's class interested in pursuing the idea privately, in your own homes, as an outside source of fun.

3. **My child could never be in chorus/band/orchestra.** Oftentimes with performance groups, the "standing still and paying attention" part is a bigger deal than the actual musical ability part. Yet there may be ways to accommodate your

child's weakness to allow her strengths to shine through. Having an aide available to prompt your child may help or maybe an older and steadier student can be assigned to that role.

Keep In Mind

Worried about your child being the only special-education student in a club full of regular-education kids he doesn't know very well? Recruit familiar companionship. Just as typical students join the organizations their friends are involved with, work with the teacher to reach out to parents in your child's class or on his special-education track so that they can join a group as a group. If the mainstream gathering in question turns out to be inappropriate for their needs, use the contacts you've made to start a separate get-together, either inside of school or out. Since children with special needs often don't have the same variety of social outlets as their typical peers, having a club of their own can be an empowering experience.

24 Attend School Activities with Your Child

Football games. School plays. Spring concerts. Homecoming parades. Are you and your child faces in those crowds? If you've been skipping these events, or attending them only with your regular-education children, you're missing out on an opportunity to strengthen your child's school experience.

Like joining clubs, attending school activities is one of those things nobody puts a lot of emphasis on for children in special education. They're bused in, bused out, and may have little contact with school outside of that—unless you make an effort to make it different. If your child is a member of the student body, he should be a member of the student body with full privileges and full presence.

That doesn't mean you drag that poor child to everything. You pick things there's a chance she may enjoy, and you're prepared to ditch out early if things don't work out. You make an appearance. You see and are seen. And maybe you'll be surprised at just what your child is able to appreciate and tolerate and sit through.

Among other things, these outings give your child an opportunity to practice social skills and behavioral strategies in a variety of environments. It does so in a way that you can personally control; unlike field trips and school assemblies, here you're able to pick and choose the event, and make sure your child has what you consider to be adequate support and management for a successful outing.

Best of all, this is happening in a place where you'll be noticed by school personnel, and that can buy you some credibility in school meetings and planning sessions. Things you do outside of school may be your word only, but if people have witnessed your child's presence at the show or the workshop or the dance, you have a stronger platform from which to say some things are working and some things aren't.

It also gives your child shared experiences with other students and professionals that can pay off in everything from speech sessions to casual conversations in the hallways. And it gives you some school contacts—if you want to gain admission for your child into a club or performing group, it helps to have seen them in action.

It's all part of establishing yourself as an interested, involved, approachable parent, with a child who's making an effort to expand his horizons. That's not a bad return on the price of a football admission or a play ticket.

Five Good Reasons to Do It
1. Your child gets exposure to different sorts of events.
2. Your child sees that school is something that's important to you.

3. Your child gets to show off her school to you a little bit.
4. Unlike events that happen during the school day, you can control these experiences for the maximum success for your child.
5. You might enjoy yourself and learn something, too.

Three Bad Reasons Not To

1. **My child isn't interested in that stuff.** What stuff is that? The stuff your child has never been to or experienced? Easy enough not to be interested in that. Expose your child to things first, then decide what's interesting and what's not.
2. **I'm not interested in that stuff.** Hey, parenting's about sacrifice. And of all the sacrifices you're going to be called upon to make, going to something boring with your kid is relatively small potatoes.
3. **I'd love to, but I don't have the time.** Fair enough . . . as long as you don't have time for this stuff for your other kids, nieces and nephews, professional sports teams, or any of those other events that may exclude your child. I'm not saying you have to go to every football game or chaperone every dance, but pick a thing or two and try it.

Keep In Mind

By the time your child hits the teenage years, the issue of school dances may arise. Your teen may want to go, or those who work with your teen may feel your teen should want to go, and you should make it happen. For many children with special needs, a couple of hours of totally unstructured time in a dark, sweaty, ear-splittingly loud place isn't exactly a formula for success. But if you do want to give it a try, sign up to chaperone. Get a few parents who know your child to sign up as well, or recruit some friends or family members. Check with the school personnel in charge and explain that this is an experiment, and if there are any problems you want to know about it. Then be available to help your child make a quick getaway if the sensory overload proves too much. For your child, that is, not you!

25 Know Your Child's Therapy Schedule

If your child has an IEP, much thought has likely gone into his particular needs for speech, occupational, and physical therapy. Your child has probably undergone lengthy evaluations to pinpoint her level of delay and inability, and requirements have been placed in that educational plan to provide intensive assistance toward meeting goals in those areas. A specific number of sessions has been assigned for each therapy, with an indication of whether sessions are to be private or group, in-class or pull-outs.

That's the easy part.

The hard part *should* be the work your child does. All too often, though, the hard part is actually getting the therapy sessions the school set you up for.

It's not so much that the school wants to foil your child's ability to write well or speak well or walk down the hallway without bumping into things. It's often more a matter of limitations: limited availability of therapists to do the job, limited space for setting up therapy rooms, limited time in test-heavy schedules for kids to be out of class. Juggling therapy schedules—making sure the right kids are in the right room at the right times with the right therapist—can be a massive undertaking, one that usually doesn't start until the beginning of the school year and so right away delays the onset of work.

The one advantage schools have is that it's very hard for parents to know when their children are supposed to be going to therapy, and when those sessions have not been provided. It's sometimes months before Mom and Dad realize that the promised therapy has not been put in place, and by that time, the powers-that-be may hope they'll have a solution.

They can't fool you, though—you're going to ask for a schedule right from the get-go. And if they haven't got one, you're going to keep politely inquiring. Ask the therapist. Ask your IEP team. Ask the person in charge of that particular type of therapy for the district or the person in charge of special education. Each answer you get, you're going to jot down on that contact log we talked about. Each time you get a "We don't know yet," you're going to ask for a deadline, and then follow up on it.

Once the therapy actually does kick in, use your knowledge of the schedule to talk to your child about it, send notes to the therapist, and arrange to sit in on therapy from time to time. And keep up a dialog with the teacher over how the therapy is working out—whether it's disrupting class time, or needs to focus on something new, or, as happens too often, stopped sometime after it started. At which point, you go back to the beginning.

Five Good Reasons to Do It

1. You make sure your child is getting the therapy that was agreed to.

2. You can talk to your child about therapy on the day it happens.

3. You know when to contact the therapist, who may not be in the school all day every day.

4. You'll know which subjects your child is missing during therapy pull-outs.

5. Hey, you're curious about your child's school day, aren't you?

Three Bad Reasons Not To

1. **I can't get a straight answer on that.** Keep asking. Politely. Persistently. With follow-up. You will, if nothing else, have a compelling record of the fact that services were not provided nor coordinated competently, and that the authorities were evasive.

2. **If the school can't get good help, that's that.** Actually, that's their cue to pay for your child to get therapy from a private therapist. If the IEP specifies therapy, the district is legally obligated to provide it. Even if you don't want to turn the screws on your fellow taxpayers, staying informed on scheduling problems at least prompts you to seek out private help to pay for yourself.

3. **I'm not sure my child even needs that therapy anyway.**
   Great! Bring it up at your planning meetings. Talk to a current therapist or, if no such personage exists, a past therapist. Get your child's name out of the problem pile if the help's not needed. But if it is, don't you give up.

Keep In Mind

That carefully maintained list of conversations and contacts regarding missing therapy can be your ticket to summer services. Make sure you keep track of how many sessions are missed, and once therapy gets rolling, ask the school how they intend to make those lost sessions up. One option will be to double up on sessions during the school day, which unacceptably causes your child to miss too much class. Instead, negotiate to get that time during the summer, or at least after school.

26　Sit In on a Therapy Session

Quick: What does your child do in therapy?

Could you replicate that at home during a school break?

Do you know what you could do to reinforce those therapy activities at home?

While most of us have a reference for what a school day is like, what goes on between your child and the school therapist is a mystery. And while back-to-school nights and teacher conferences can clue you in to your child's particular classroom experience in any given year, there's no Therapy Open House to clue you in on what speech therapy or occupational therapy or physical therapy looks like.

But if you ask, you can probably get a look.

Talk to the therapist—or, if you can't manage to get a hold of that individual, try your caseworker instead—about setting up a visit to observe your child in therapy. The therapist should welcome the opportunity to meet you and to show you what your child does during these sessions. Some things to consider during your observation:

- Where does it take place?
- Is the room large enough and free from distractions?

- ▶ Does the therapist have all of the furnishings and equipment necessary?
- ▶ Who is in your child's therapy group?
- ▶ Do those other students seem to have similar needs to your child?
- ▶ Does your child participate as fully as the other students?
- ▶ Are your child's needs met in a group setting?
- ▶ Is this a good time of day for your child?
- ▶ Is your child tired or distracted or upset to be missing class?
- ▶ Does the therapist have a good rapport with your child?
- ▶ Does your child seem to enjoy the therapy session?
- ▶ Are there things your child is asked to do during therapy that he seems to be afraid of or resistant to?

If you see problems in any area, discuss them with the therapist. Then, if there are things that need to be changed or concerns that need to be reconciled, take them to your case manager or the person in the district in charge of that type of therapy. Maybe changes can be made and maybe they can't; but if you've observed and commented and documented your conversations, you'll be in a strong position at the next IEP meeting to attribute lack of progress to identified problems, and include language in the IEP to address that.

Five Good Reasons to Do It

1. It's a good way to meet the therapist.
2. It's easier to talk to your child about therapy if you know what goes on there.
3. You can spot problems early.
4. You'll learn more about the ways therapy can help your child.
5. You may pick up some tips for how to help your child at home.

Three Bad Reasons Not To

1. **I'm not available at the time my child has therapy.** Ask if, for this one time, the therapy could be rescheduled. One possibility might be to bring your child before or after school for a special observation session. This may not be feasible if your child has group therapy, but for one-on-ones, it may be doable. If the therapist is one who travels from school to school, you may have to be willing to go where she's at on the day you're available. You won't be able to see your child's normal therapy room, but at least you'll get a look at how the therapist works.

2. **I don't want to embarrass my child in front of a therapy group.** More likely, the other kids will be jealous that your child has a parent who comes to observe. Assuming you're

going to behave yourself and not fuss over your child, it should be fine.

3. **The school says it's not allowed.** If this is the line you're getting, you should know that in very many school districts, parent observation is indeed allowed, and even encouraged. Therapists are usually glad to meet and interact with parents, if it can be done in a nondisruptive way. If your school doesn't encourage that, maybe you should start wondering what they're trying to hide.

Keep In Mind

If your child's behavior takes a nosedive when you're on the premises, you're going to have a hard time really observing what a therapy session is like when you're not around. But don't let that keep you away—the therapist should be able to come up with an activity that can include you, giving you a nice opportunity to see what your child does and have some fun. And at the very least, you'll see how the therapist deals with your child during stressful times.

27   Send In a Communication Notebook for Therapists

As with the teacher, knowing what the therapist is doing with your child and how well it's going is an important way of supporting your child's school experience. Since therapists work with a variety of students on complicated schedules, sometimes at a number of schools around the district, they can be hard to track down by phone. E-mail is a possibility, but a better way of keeping in constant easy communication is by sending a notebook with your child for just that purpose.

The therapist can jot a few notes in the book each time your child has a session, which has the added advantage of letting you know that sessions actually did take place. You can jot down observations of things that have been happening at home that may be of interest to the therapist. And the two of you can exchange questions and answers in one coordinated place.

If your child's speech therapist regularly gives homework, you may already be getting a notebook home to facilitate that, and you can use it to exchange comments and questions as well. For other therapists, you can purchase an inexpensive small composition book at an office-supply store to serve the purpose. Mark it with the type of therapy on front, as well as your child's name and the therapist's name.

Sending the book in is no problem—making sure it gets to the therapy session, and then gets back to you, may be. If your child has trouble keeping track of such things, ask the teacher or aide to make sure that the book goes along to therapy and then makes it back into the book bag. They may not remember every time, but getting the grownups involved means there's a higher likelihood you'll see that small volume than if it's only your child in charge of it. You may want to keep the communication notebook at home and send it in on the days your child has therapy; if it doesn't come home on those days, ask about it.

Most likely, one communication notebook will be enough to see you through the school year. When you see a book getting close to the end, though, go ahead and replace it. You're more likely to keep a constant flow of communication going if you provide the medium for conducting it.

Five Good Reasons to Do It

1. You'll keep on top of what's happening in therapy.
2. You'll get confirmation that the therapy is happening as scheduled.
3. You can ask questions and get quick answers.

4. It's hard to stay in touch with therapists any other way, since they're often at different schools at different times on different days.

5. You'll have a handy record of your child's therapy progress for use in planning meetings.

Three Bad Reasons Not To

1. **I'll just e-mail the therapist instead.** And that's not a bad idea either. The advantage of the communication book, though, is that the therapist will have it right there while your child is right there. Instead of having to remember what went on in a session, or having to remember what your e-mail said while the session is taking place, all the communication will be at hand and on the spot, with a built-in time to write back. You can always e-mail too, for clarification and further discussion.

2. **I can never think of anything to write.** No pressure. If it winds up just containing reports from the therapist, that's a significant advantage. And if neither of you can think of anything to write, at least ask the therapist to write down the day your child was seen and initial it. That's a useful record right there.

3. **My child's too old to be bringing communication books back and forth.** It does seem sort of like something a

kindergarten teacher would distribute. Still, it's a useful and necessary thing, and not by definition something kiddish. If it helps, have your child pick out some cool notebooks to use for the note exchange or decorate the communication book with graffiti or cartoons.

Keep In Mind

Be sure to bring your communication notebooks along when you go to meetings the therapists will be attending. Having a concrete record of concerns or triumphs, things tried or problems solved, in the therapist's very own words and writing, is a good way to make sure everybody is on the right page. You may feel it's kind of a "gotcha" move, but the therapists will probably be just as glad to have a reminder, since they see so many students in so little time and can't reasonably remember everything. If it feels better, review the notes in a private meeting with the therapist before a larger meeting.

28   Talk with Your Child about Therapy

One of the advantages of using a communication notebook with your child's therapists is that it gives you some material for those conversations you're having with your child on the subject.

Unless . . . maybe your child reports back consistently about therapy, in useful detail and at great conversational length, without any prompting from you?

Yeah, mine never did, either.

Talking to your child about therapy can give you some insight into what he finds fun and what he finds frightening. It can help you understand which therapist she likes and which she doesn't, or which class he hates to miss. Your child may not volunteer the information that therapy sessions have not been taking place, but if you have an empty book to ask about, the truth's more likely to come out.

With the help of those back-and-forth notes, your experience of observing therapy, and your knowledge of the therapy schedule, you're armed to make useful chats happen. On a day when you know your child is supposed to have had therapy, ask about it: "Did you have speech today?"

You may get a yeah or a no. You may get some information on how it was earlier or later than usual, or somebody was absent.

Ask if your child did something you know she enjoyed when you observed the therapy, or that the therapist has told you about. Ask about less desirable activities. Have your child tell you three fun things he did or three things that were hard.

Just by *having* this conversation, you're supporting all that speech therapy—and maybe getting your child a little more interested and involved in the other things she gets pulled out to do each day.

If your child tells you a sweet or funny story about something that happened in therapy or describes something in a darling way, be sure to jot it in the communication notebook. Therapists work hard with children who often don't give a lot back, and they deserve every "aw" and "ha!" they can get.

Of course, if your child is talking about things that aren't so great, you'll want to touch base with the therapist about those, too. Sometimes, it's a part of therapy to stretch what your child can tolerate, and he may be asked to do things that are unpleasant and undesirable and scary (like put his hands in something sticky or walk on a balance beam). Your child's unhappiness with a particular therapy session is not necessarily a sign that something's wrong, but the therapist will want to know that your child felt strongly enough about what was going on to relay that information back to you.

Five Good Reasons to Do It

1. You'll have some good together-time with your child.
2. You'll support the therapy by drawing your child out about it.
3. Any type of talk strengthens speech skills.
4. You may hear some cute things that will make you smile.
5. You may hear some not-so-cute things you'll want to check into.

Three Bad Reasons Not To

1. **My child won't talk to me about that.** Certainly your child's not going to volunteer information, and it may be that any conversation on the subject will be largely one-sided. But if you can include in your side enough details about what really goes on in therapy, it may unearth some interesting tidbits on your child's side.
2. **I can never keep track of when therapy is.** Well, that's something *you* can change. Note it on your calendar. Put it in your computer alerts. Set your cell phone to send you a message. Keep that therapy schedule at the top level of your attention, so that you know when the time is right to discuss it.
3. **My child only complains, and I hate to hear it.** Two possibilities here: The therapy really is awful; in that case, you

have to do something about it. Or the therapy's mostly okay, but your kid's a whiner. In that case, you need to use the information you've gained to draw her out on things that are less awful. Either way, gotta talk about it.

Keep In Mind

Your child is in therapy because something important is difficult. So therapy isn't going to be all lollipops and roses. It's going to be hard, and it should be. A good therapist will find a way to wrap that hard stuff in layers and layers of games and goo and goofiness, and if that's not happening—to a degree that your child can't fully gain the benefits of therapy—you'll need to look into it. But don't be too discouraged if your child complains. And don't be too suspicious if it sounds like all he does is play.

29 Know What the Therapy Is Supposed to Accomplish

You sign off on your child's therapy goals every time you sign an IEP. But do you really have a clue what all that stuff about graphomotor skills and visual/perceptual skills and positioning and body awareness and auditory processing and other big terms the therapists throw around really mean?

Talking with the OT and the PT and the speech therapist about those goals and what achieving them will mean to your child is an important step to supporting the therapy at home. You want to make sure that your expectations are realistic, and you want to be able to assess progress. That's hard to do when you don't know what to expect or where your child is headed.

It might also be worth asking your therapists to recommend some books to help you understand the type of therapy your child is getting and what it can be expected to accomplish. Do some research on terms that are confusing to you, and ask around online or in-person support groups to find out what sort of services other kids are getting.

Use that knowledge to evaluate your child's goals. Do they address the problems you see when your child does homework? Do they deal with difficulties your child struggles with in gym class, or recess, or walking down the halls? Is assistance being provided for penmanship problems, difficulty sitting upright, language weaknesses? If you see goals that seem to be there for the sake of keeping your child busy or goals that you feel have already been accomplished, point that out. And if there are items of great importance that are missing, point those out, too. An IEP is always a work in progress, and changes can be made—or you can work out an informal arrangement with the therapist to work on some side goals the two of you agree on.

Keep track of those IEP goals as the school year goes on, and think about whether you've seen improvement. Consider whether problems that have been reported with classroom performance and behavior may be related to the shortcomings addressed in the goals, and recruit the therapist to help you advocate for your child. Therapy shouldn't be something that is isolated from the rest of the school day, and once you understand how everything fits together, you'll be able to act as a force for integration.

Five Good Reasons to Do It
1. You have an obligation to understand your child's IEP.
2. Once you "get" the goals, you can help fine-tune or change them.

3. What you learn may make a difference for your child at home, too.

4. It will help you advocate for your child and for the therapists, too.

5. Learning new concepts is good for your brain.

Three Bad Reasons Not To

1. **I trust the therapists to know what they're doing.** Trust is a wonderful thing, and a terrific spirit to bring to special-education interactions. But blind trust? Not so great. Show the people you're working with the respect of caring about what they do.

2. **That stuff is too confusing.** It's really not. You just have to get somebody to explain it to you in small, normal-person words. Keep asking questions until you get some answers you can wrap your mind around. If your child's therapist can't do that, ask to speak to the person who's in charge of that therapy for your school district.

3. **Those school goals are the school's business.** But your child is your business. If she's not getting everything she should from an activity that's pulling her out of class, you should know about it. And if he's getting punished in class for something related to that therapy, you should know about that, too. These parts of your child don't exist in separate

compartments; they overlap messily, and you're the one in the best position to see the big picture.

Keep In Mind

If it's feasible for you financially, your child may benefit from having sessions with a private therapist on top of whatever she's getting in school. The private work can address problems outside of school that are impacted by your child's delays and disabilities. And since you're the one paying the bill, you're more likely to get a detailed answer when you ask just what exactly is going on with all of this. Put the private therapist in touch with the school therapist to coordinate the work being done in both places. While it may not be easy to get insurance to pay for the type of therapy your child needs, there are sometimes billing codes that the therapist or your doctor may know about that can help. Ask around as you choose a private therapist to see if they have some tricks for this.

30   Ask the Therapists about Issues at Home

Your child's IEP is really only supposed to address issues that directly impact on schoolwork—the language needed for classroom participation, handwriting ability, physical skills for gym class, that sort of thing. As an instrument for providing your child with a Free and Appropriate Public Education, it's not particularly concerned with how he eats or sleeps or rides a bike. Even sensory-integration therapy, though it can absolutely have an effect on your child's ability to sit still at a desk, is an iffy proposition for a lot of school districts.

So your child's therapy goals are liable to be very specific to things that can be identified as school needs, and you may be told in no uncertain terms that this is the way things have to be, by law, case closed. Respect that, insofar as the planning meeting goes. Then snag the therapist in a private conversation, drop some words in her ear about what you'd like help with, and see if you can't make some sort of informal arrangement to address those not-ready-for-school-time issues.

It may be that your child's at-home needs can be folded into something that's already being done to facilitate official goals. Possibly, the therapist can just add something to the routine without doing it officially. A therapist who's experienced in sensory integration may well just go ahead and include that as part of the therapy—I've had both occupational and physical therapists do their jobs with a sensory-integration slant.

At the very least, that therapist you've been building a relationship with through the communication book and the therapy observations (you have been, right?) may be able to provide you with some demonstrations of things you can do at home or may point you toward books with activities for parents.

Your therapist may actually know, just through working with your child, what sorts of things are likely to be issues at home. She may have worked with similar kids and provided assistance, so she might have some help all ready to go, just for the asking. You do have to ask, though. You can acknowledge all over the place that you know this isn't actually the therapist's job and you're imposing. If it's a bother, you'll get told that.

But why not try? In the end, the strengths your child gains at home will improve his school abilities, as the stresses he experiences there detract from them. The better the therapist knows your child in all environments, the more effective the therapy will be. A good therapist should be eager to collaborate with you on that project.

Five Good Reasons to Do It

1. You may get some much-needed assistance on home issues.
2. It will help you form a collaborative team with the therapist.
3. It will broaden the therapist's knowledge and understanding of your child.
4. Things that reduce your child's stress at home will make classroom behavior better, too.
5. Hey, it's your tax dollars paying for those school services. Why not get everything from them you can?

Three Bad Reasons Not To

1. **I've been told the therapists can only deal with school goals.** Who told you that? If it was the therapist, then you probably do have to back off. But if it was anybody else, go ahead and approach the therapist anyway. The worst she can say is no.
2. **I have private therapy for our home goals.** Great! But having those reinforced at school (and school goals reinforced in private therapy) won't hurt. Check in with the school therapist about it, anyway.
3. **I don't want anyone to know we have problems at home.** Here's a little secret: If you have the kind of kid who has problems at home that you don't want anyone to know

about, chances are the people at school know about it. Your child isn't one person at home and a completely different individual at school. Asking for advice and assistance means you're on top of the situation and doing what you can to rectify it. That should be considered a positive thing, not a black mark on your permanent record.

Keep In Mind

Just as you can seek advice from the therapist on the best way to work with your child, you can give advice right back. If you've found something that works well, share that information. If your child has done something difficult or surprising or cute, tell the tale. Always remember that, while the therapists who work with your child are experts in speech and language pathology, occupational therapy, or physical therapy, you are the foremost expert on the life and development of your particular unique youngster. They need your expertise as much as you need theirs. Don't hesitate to step up.

31   Offer to Provide Needed Therapy or Educational Materials

So your child needs a special seat cushion. A pencil grip. A weighted vest. Fidget toys.

If these tools are needed for school-mandated therapy, the school district should provide them. And maybe it will, if you've got time to wait—for meetings, for authorizations, for requisitions, for ordering, for delivering, for packages making their way from some central mailroom to your school, your therapist, your child.

That could honestly take months. In fact, items strategized about early in a school year may not make it in much before June.

Does your child have that kind of time? Chances are, he needs what he needs when he needs it. Fortunately, there's an alternative to waiting, patiently, helplessly.

Buy the stuff yourself.

It's easy to think of equipment used by speech therapists, occupational therapists, physical therapists, adaptive gym instructors, and classroom teachers as only available through some top-secret Educator Emporium unavailable to parents. But in fact, most of this stuff can be ordered through mail-order catalogs and online sources, and you'll get it way quicker with your credit card than the professionals can with their purchase orders. Some things you may even be able to get at the local toy store.

Teachers do this all the time, sadly. When you're having those friendly conversations with your child's teacher, ask where her supplies come from. Most likely, your child's educators drop a significant amount of their own money at school-supply stores getting those special notebooks or decorations or writing instruments. They need what they need when they need it, too.

So chip in. Find out what the therapists need to work effectively with your child. Inquire as to what they would do if they had the right tools. Quiz the teacher on things she's seen kids use in the past that might well serve your child. And then, do some shopping.

If cost is not a concern, you can have yourself a pretty sweet shopping spree at some of these therapy-product places, finding things that may help you out at home, too. A set of pencil grips or wrist weights can be spread out for use in a number of places—home, school, private therapy sessions.

On the other hand, if the price tag is too steep, you may be able to spread the cost over a number of families. Ask your therapist if there are other parents whose children need the same things, and contact them about sharing the goodies and splitting the cost.

Some items you may even be able to make or improvise yourself. Line the pockets of a vest with curtain weights to make a weighted vest, or fill a balloon with sand for a makeshift squeeze toy. If you or your spouse are particularly handy with tools, you may be able to build your own customized balance beam or a footrest.

Eventually, your child may outgrow a particular tool, either physically or developmentally. When that time comes, if a younger sibling can't use it, be generous and donate the item to the therapist or teacher. It's a good feeling to know that something that helped your child will help other children, and you may be in a position to benefit from someone else's generosity down the line.

Five Good Reasons to Do It

1. You make sure the right equipment is purchased.
2. You get it and give it, so you know it got there.
3. Your child gets needed help in a timely fashion.
4. You may be able to spread the good fortune to other kids in need.
5. You get a reputation for being a helpful parent.

Three Bad Reasons Not To

1. **It's not right—the district should pay!** Yes, indeed it should. In fact, the district should do lots of things it doesn't, most of them hard to do yourself instead. This one is easy. Choose your battles.

2. **I wouldn't know what to get.** Ask your child's therapist for a shopping list, and show him what you're planning to get before putting out the bucks.

3. **I wouldn't know where to get it.** Appendix C at the back of this book offers information on sites to order from. Or ask your child's therapist for some recommended catalogs or local shops.

Keep in Mind

When sending in items that you've purchased for school use, write your child's name and school in permanent ink somewhere easy to see. Many therapists travel from school to school and may not have reliable storage, and it's not impossible that, even with good will and intentions, items will go astray. You'll want to be able to prove what's yours. And if you wind up donating the item at some point? You'll want people to know who to thank.

32 Request Suggestions for Continuing Therapy at Home

We've looked at how important homework is for reinforcing schoolwork and keeping you on top of strengths and weaknesses.

It should be no surprise, then, that homework's an important part of your child's therapy work as well.

Still, though it ought to be a given, you may have to ask therapists to send homework. That communication notebook you've been exchanging would be one way to do it, or informal conversations or e-mails suggesting areas in which practice might make perfect.

You're probably most likely to get homework sent home from speech therapists, since the things they do require the least specialized equipment, and look the most like traditional homework. Take those assignments seriously when they come home with your child, and make sure they're not forgotten in the rush to complete academic work. If there's a problem with completing them, contact the therapist just as you would the teacher with a homework problem.

And if you wonder how having your child blow on a cotton ball or pick up Cheerios with her tongue applies to speech therapy, ask the therapist about that, too.

If improving graphomotor skills (that's handwriting to you and me) is one of your child's occupational-therapy goals, he's doing "homework" for that when he does homework for everything else. Working on physical therapy skills might be as simple as playing a game of catch or taking a trip to the playground. A therapist addressing sensory integration may advise you to brush your child's skin with a surgical scrub brush or provide experiences like trampoline jumping or ball-pit diving.

Your therapists should be happy to provide you with home-reinforcement ideas for the asking. So ask. You'll show your support for the work that's being done and help it get done faster. As with all the homework your child does, make some notes of what you do together and how it's going. Share any struggles or triumphs with the therapist. Follow through with what you're asked to do and report back. And use the observations you've recorded when it comes time to evaluate your child's progress for the year and plan goals for the year to come.

And oh yeah, have fun with it. Unlike most homework, there's usually an element of play or socializing between you and your child in these therapy assignments. You get credit for both homework *and* "quality time" here. That's a bargain you're not going to want to pass up.

Five Good Reasons to Do It

1. Therapy homework will probably be more fun than normal homework.

2. As with everything else, more practice means more progress.
3. You'll learn more about your child's weaknesses and strengths.
4. You'll build on your collaborative relationship with the therapist.
5. You'll have something to share around the IEP table.

Three Bad Reasons Not To

1. **My child has too much homework already.** The nice thing is that a lot of therapy homework provides a good and refreshing break from academic desk work. Your child can think it's play—the homework part will be your secret.
2. **I'm no therapist.** You're probably not a professional teacher, either, but that doesn't keep you from helping with homework. Therapy homework's the same thing—you're reinforcing activities and goals that have already been introduced at school.
3. **I don't understand how this stuff works.** Don't try to understand the science or theory behind it. If you can, that's great, and working with your child may make you want to learn more about the therapies that are being done. But unlike algebra or science, with therapy homework, you can pretty much just follow directions and let it go at that.

Keep In Mind

You don't have to rely solely on your child's therapists to provide reinforcing work for home. There are plenty of resources available to help parents work with their kids. Books and sites that can help you create your own "homework" include:

- The Out-of-Sync Child Has Fun: Activities for Kids with Sensory Integration Dysfunction *by Carol Stock Kranowitz*
- How Does Your Engine Run? A Leader's Guide to the Alert Program for Self-Regulation *by Mary Sue Williams and Sherry Shellenberger*
- T.A.S.C.: Tools for Achieving Social Confidence *by Sandra Furia and Jennifer DiTrani*
- Teach Me How to Say It Right: Helping Your Child with Articulation Problems *by Dorothy P. Dougherty*
- What Did You Say? What Do You Mean? An Illustrated Guide for Understanding Metaphors *by Jude Welton, illustrated by Jane Telford*
- Starting Sensory Integration Therapy: Fun Activities That Won't Destroy Your Home or Classroom *by Bonnie Arnwine*
- Brain Gym: Simple Activities for Whole Brain Learning *by Paul E. Dennison and Gail E. Dennison*
- *Handwriting Without Tears*–www.hwtears.com/parents/newtohwt
- *Play Activities*–http://play-activities.com
- *Autism Games*–http://autismgames.googlepages.com

33　Know Your Child's Bus Route and Companions

There's a place your child spends a significant percentage of her school day that's never a part of open houses or classroom visits. She sees the people there more than her therapists, but they don't get to participate in her IEP planning. They don't even get a copy of the IEP document.

That place in which your child spends so much unregulated time is the school bus, and those people are the bus driver and aide. These individuals have an unsung impact on your child's school day, and they can truly make a difference in your child's stress level in the morning and afternoon. It makes sense that you should know each other as more than a hand waving from a window.

That's not easy, because probably the only time you're going to see them is when they're on the job. The last thing they need is some parent chatting them up when they've got a bus full of jittery students and a schedule to keep. But there are things you can do during that morning hand-off that will help.

Learning the names of the persons to whom you trust the care of your child on the road is a good start. Introduce yourself on the first day of school or at the first opportunity, and exchange greetings in the morning as your child boards the bus. Go down to the bus with your child and make yourself available in case the bus personnel have comments, complaints, or cute stories to share.

While you're at it, get a look at the kids who are on the bus with your child. You may be able to talk it over with your child and learn the names of the bus mates that way, and you may even recognize many of them from your child's class. Or you may be able to ask the bus aide who the other children are, once you're on a friendly footing.

If you don't mind looking like a little bit of a loon, follow the bus one morning to see the route and who gets picked up where. Then drive it again with your child, and have her point out the houses they stop at and tell you who gets on. You may get an early warning of problems aboard, or find out who lives close enough to you to be potential play-date material. That route is a major part of your child's morning routine, and something you can easily share.

Five Good Reasons to Do It

1. You need to know who you're entrusting your child to.
2. Bus personnel don't get a lot of respect. Give them some.
3. Learning about bus time can lead to good conversations with your child.

4. Learning the bus route can help you evaluate if it's too long.
5. Being an interested, involved parent should extend to every second your child's away from you, not just classroom time.

Three Bad Reasons Not To

1. **I'm not dressed when my child leaves in the morning.** Oh, come on, throw on a pair of sweats or something. No one cares if you have your makeup on or your hair combed. You don't really want to place your vanity ahead of your child's safety and happiness, do you? (All right, if it's that important to look your best, get out of bed a little earlier so that you can be both present and presentable.)

2. **The bus people don't seem very friendly.** And so . . . you're afraid of them, but you put your child on their bus anyway? Make an effort. Be a cheerful greeter. If the adults on the bus seem particularly gruff or mean, that's something you're going to want to be asking your child about on a regular basis and monitoring with other parents. But more likely, if you make an effort, you can break the ice.

3. **I took a bus when I was a kid, and my parents never had anything to do with it.** But the bus your child is taking is different, isn't it, and the bus aide in particular has a responsibility that isn't found on "normal" buses. Your child's different, too, and needs your protection and concern. Parents

have the most opportunity of anyone on the IEP team to relay concerns and needs to those before- and after-school monitors. Do your job.

Keep In Mind

When you're planning gifts for teachers and therapists at holiday time or the end of the year, don't forget those grownups who spend so much time with your child on the way to and from school. A small remembrance—even just some cookies you've made with your child—shows that you value and appreciate the work they do, and consider them an important part of your child's day.

34   Look for Bus-Related School Problems

Remember the "stress speedometer"? Way back in Chapter 1, we talked about how small things happening early in the day can nudge the needle and cause a blowout later on. Just as that goes for your morning routine, it goes for the bus ride, too.

That's a whole lot of unstructured time your child is spending in that vehicle, boring time, maybe stressful time if another child is out of control or an adult is unsympathetic. Think about how long your child spends on that bus, and about how you would feel after a ride like that. Fresh and ready to start learning? Maybe not so much.

When misbehaviors arise during the school day, and teachers do a behavior analysis to try to find the cause, make sure that bus time is among the places they're going to look. In addition to that, consider the time between when your child gets off the bus and when he goes to class. Does she hang out in a big noisy gym with lots of other barely supervised kids? Does he have to stand outside in the cold or the heat? Does she wait with a small group under an aide's supervision? Is it a long wait? These are factors you as a parent might not ever really think about, but they can have a significant impact on your child's behavior and learning readiness.

Keep on top of the bus situation as best you can. Make sure the bus aide and driver know they can approach you with problems, without having to go through official channels. Thank them by not overreacting when they complain about something your child is doing. Work collaboratively to think of things that will help, and only go higher in the chain of command when you run out of other options—or, preferably, when you all agree it's necessary.

Similarly, if the downtime your child spends between bus and school, and school and bus, are causing stress and presenting the opportunity for trouble, talk to the teacher or your case manager about what can be done. There may be other options available, and surely it's better for all concerned if those options are put into effect before disaster strikes rather than after.

Be particularly aware of how long before school your child is being picked up, and where all that time is going. Is the district trying to economize by putting too many children on one bus, regardless of how far-flung their homes are? Is your child arriving at school too early, or even worse, too late? Do the math, ask the questions, and make a stand. Chances are nobody—not the bus personnel, not the teachers—is happy with the way things are. Show your support by caring.

Five Good Reasons to Do It

1. This represents a big chunk of your child's day, so it's important.
2. No one else is thinking very much about it.
3. Bullies and boredom are big problems for kids with special needs, and the bus is a prime spot for both.
4. Often, these problems are simple to fix.
5. This is one of the few services your child gets that you could provide yourself if necessary.

Three Bad Reasons Not To

1. **The bus people say there's nothing to do about it.** Sure they do, because they don't want you to complain. But this is a service provided under the IEP, and the service provider should therefore be receptive to input from parents. Put some in.
2. **I don't want to make any trouble for my child.** The idea here is to take trouble from your child. If you pursue your concerns in a respectful and collaborative way, with an accent on making things easier for all the professionals involved, you should be able to have some positive, trouble-free impact.
3. **How am I supposed to know what goes on in that bus?** You're supposed to ask. And once you do, you may be

surprised how willing teachers and aides and drivers are to share their complaints and concerns with you.

Keep In Mind

Bus service can be tremendously helpful to parents whose children are being bused out of the neighborhood, and have other kids to get to school or jobs to go to. Bus rides are often fun and useful to kids who need a transition from home to school or enjoy the social opportunities the bus brings. If neither of these is a factor for your family and child, though, think seriously about whether the bus is the best way for your student to get to school. Just because it's offered doesn't mean you have to take it. Providing "bus" service yourself may give your child enough extra time in the a.m. or p.m. to be worth the inconvenience.

35 Look for Lunch-Related School Problems

So how's mealtime with your child at home? A peaceful garden of culinary delight? A time for chats and good fellowship? Or a minefield of thrown food, silverware struggles, food refusals, and silent chewing? If the answer's closer to that last one rather than the first two, don't expect that your child's school lunchtime is going to be miraculously free from strife.

Lunchtime doesn't get much discussion in IEP meetings, but it can make a big difference in your child's school experience. Anxiety about it can derail a morning, repercussions from a bad cafeteria time can ripple through an afternoon, and socializing with classmates can be tough for the kid who can't wield a fork or get with the gossip or chew with his mouth closed.

Start by finding out who's in charge of your child during that midday meal. Does an aide or teacher keep close watch? Are there any adults directing activity at all? Do kids sit in assigned groups or with whomever they choose? Are bullies policed or allowed to roam?

Speak to the individual who's responsible for your child at mealtime—or, if there is no such person, to the teacher or case manager. Share your concerns about your child's eating oddities.

If fork work is a problem, consider skipping the school hot lunch and sending something from home. There's plenty of finger-food that's perfectly acceptable for lunchtimes—a good old-fashioned sandwich, carrots, and an apple, for starters. Your child may need to work on that fine-motor fork control with the occupational therapist, but not in a lunchroom in front of peers.

Scheduling therapy during lunchtime may actually be a good solution if bullying or anxiety is killing your child's appetite in the cafeteria. Other options may include a lunchtime club that moves meals into a classroom, or even going home for lunch. These are exceptions that would have to be negotiated with your case manager and school administration, but if they have the effect of removing behavior problems and making your child a happier student, they may be worth it. Worth asking about, anyway.

One quick way to support your child at lunchtime that requires no collaboration from school personnel at all is slipping a note in her lunch. Just a quick encouraging phrase—"I love you!" "Hope you're having a good day!" "I'm thinking of you right now!" "Keep trying! I know you can do it!"—may give your child a little extra bit of pep to make it through the rest of a long, hard day. Oh, it'll be embarrassing, sure, but the value will not be lost. I know, because I sure liked it when my mom snuck them in my lunch bags.

Five Good Reasons to Do It

1. Fear of lunch can cause behavior problems in the morning.

2. Fear from lunch can cause behavior problems in the afternoon.

3. Bullies and eating habits are major problems for kids with special needs, and they're likely to be lurking at lunch.

4. Often, these problems are simple to fix.

5. Remember what a jungle the cafeteria was like when you were a kid? Now, imagine your child dealing with that.

Three Bad Reasons Not To

1. **I don't want to embarrass my child by asking for special treatment.** If the special treatment is to avoid eating problems or social problems, there's probably a greater risk of embarrassment if you don't do anything. The emphasis should be on stopping the negative experience first, then working on skills to enable a positive experience.

2. **Lunch is the least of my worries.** Okay. But it's still *a* worry. And it's still an experience that your child has in school every single day. If it's a negative experience, you may want to move it up on your list of concerns.

3. **I can't get anyone to tell me what goes on in that lunchroom.** Here's where volunteering comes in handy, because if you schedule things right, you can take a peek yourself. And

here's where building relationships with teachers and aides and therapists and other school personnel come in handy, because you can get them to tell you what they're not supposed to. Or be your spies, maybe.

Keep In Mind

Make sure you've explored all the options for money-changing in the cafeteria line. Some children with special needs have a hard time with money, and a pressured place with a bunch of jeering peers behind is not the place for experiments. Ask if the school has a program where you can pay ahead and get vouchers or a card. Alternatively, give your child exactly the amount needed each day, or close to it. You can give the teacher an envelope of extra money in case you ever forget to send the cash.

36 Know What Your Child Is Doing at Recess

Oh, man, recess. Did you love it as a kid, or see it as a treacherous no-man's-land of bullies and brats and dodge balls aimed directly at your head? I hated it when I was a kid, and have hated it on my kids' behalf since.

But there it is, still on the agenda in most elementary schools, though certainly getting shorter. And really, by all rights, recess should be a time in your child's day when he's free from restrictions and able to move and yell and relax. It ought to be a stress-busting opportunity, a bit of carefree time to fortify him for the classes ahead. Unfortunately, the playground is full of other little humans who seem determined to keep that from happening. Maybe some big humans, too.

If your child has behavior problems in the classroom, consider whether the root of the problem could be planted out in that playground. There doesn't have to be a time correlation—your child may act up in the A.M. out of stressful anticipation of High Noon, or afterward as a result of what went on. Misbehaving in a way that gets recess rescinded as a consequence may be a sign that your student is trying to avoid something (or, of course, may be the thing she wants to avoid).

It's not easy to stay on top of your child's midday routine, but it's worth asking around a little bit to see what you can learn. Does your child have supervision on the playground? Who provides it? How closely do they watch? Do they do anything *but* watch? Does anyone mediate schoolyard scuffles? Do those individuals have the needed information to treat your child fairly? Will they talk to you about any problems your child is having with playing or socializing?

Talk to those grownups. And, of course, talk to your child. Should anything mentioned concern you, bring that information to your child's teacher and case manager. There may be alternatives that can make that period more tolerable. Your child may be able to have therapy during resource time, precluding the need to go out. Aides may be able to implement a game you send in to create an organized positive recess experience. The school may be able to assign a buddy to your child or cordon off a small group of appropriate playmates.

Don't make the mistake of so many parents in all those children's novels who are completely clueless that anything bad could happen at recess, anything their child couldn't handle. Stay vigilant to every part of your student's day, even nonscholarly ones.

Five Good Reasons to Do It

1. This represents a crucial chunk of your child's day, so it's important.

2. No one else is thinking very much about it.
3. Bullies and playground games are major problems for kids with special needs, and recess is rife with them.
4. Often, these problems are simple to fix.
5. Remember what recess was like when you were a kid? Now, imagine your child dealing with that.

Three Bad Reasons Not To

1. **My child doesn't complain, so it must be okay.** Children with special needs often complain not with their words, but their behavior. Is his behavior complaining? Better make sure it's not.

2. **Surviving recess makes you tough.** That's a nice survival-of-the-fittest philosophy, and maybe it worked for you, but it stunk for me, and it will stink for your child. Chances are, your child has challenges enough without living the *Lord of the Flies* every noonday. Help out, wouldja?

3. **My child loves recess!** Terrific! I'm happy for her! Really! And let's hope it stays that way. But the only way you can make sure it stays that way is by checking up now and again. Life on the playground is constantly in flux, with peer-group allegiances shifting, bullies adjusting their targets, games gaining and waning in popularity, and the transition from accepted to ridiculed often taking place in the

blink of an eye. These are things that even regular-education students struggle with, and your child all the more so. Show some interest and support, so your child will know it's okay to come to you when problems arise.

Keep In Mind

One recess-time trouble-spot you may not ordinarily consider is the rest-rooms. They're likely to be more crowded at midday than they would be if your child goes there during class time, and that can make them a social landmine. If your child's getting into trouble in the bathroom, or being bothered there, ask if he can do his business in the restroom in the nurse's office instead. As a bonus, this is a nice way to build a friendly relationship between your child and the school nurse.

37   Check In with Your Child's Physical-Education Teacher

Another trying part of your child's day that you'll rarely hear about around the IEP table is physical education. Yet it can definitely have an impact on your child's behavior and availability for learning throughout the day. Consider some of the potential stress-spikers that time in the gym class can bring:

- Difficulty with gross-motor skills
- Teasing by other kids for being unable to do things like catching or running or kicking
- Sensitivity to loud noises in an echoing room
- Having to adjust enthusiasm for physical activity to fit with rigid rules
- It may be the only mainstreamed part of the day, so lots of strange kids around
- Gym teachers may not know about behavior plans or disabilities and, therefore, may be unsympathetic
- Low muscle tone can lead to quick tiredness that is not believed
- If gym's not scheduled every day, it's a disruption of routine

> ❯ Changing in a locker room is hard for kids with fine-motor problems

Depending on how your child feels about athletics, gym can wire her up and make it hard to slow down afterwards, wear him out and make it hard to pay attention afterwards, or stress her out and make it hard for her to calm down afterwards. Woe to the teacher of the class afterwards.

There are things you can do to help. First, find out if there's an adaptive gym class available that your child would qualify for. Adaptive gym is sort of a special-ed version of the physical-education class, with a teacher who's trained to work with children with disabilities. Ideally, this will involve adapting the activity everyone else is doing in a way that makes it accessible to your child.

If you're stuck with regular gym, talk to the teacher about your child. Provide a copy of the IEP (the teacher should have seen it, but it might just have been a glance in the case manager's office). Highlight information that applies to gym. Make sure any behavior plan is available to, and understood by, the gym teacher, and explain how this will make things easier for everyone.

Having an aide with your child in gym may help, not only to assist with activities but to remove your child from the excitement if necessary. It may also be possible to have the physical therapist do your child's session in gym class to strengthen those abilities in the environment where they'll be used. (Or, alternatively, to pull your child out for therapy so he can work on them in a more productive place.)

Supervision in the locker room will also be important; find out what's been planned for this, and check with your child regularly to make sure it's in place. Check, too, that your child can easily get into and out of gym clothes and school clothes. Work at home on any difficulties. Velcro shoes may make the difference between getting to class on time or constant lateness.

Five Good Reasons to Do It

1. This might represent an excruciating chunk of your child's day, so it's important.
2. No one else is thinking very much about it.
3. Bullies and motor skills are major problems for kids with special needs, and gym class is weighted down with them.
4. Often, these problems are simple to fix.
5. Gym teachers frequently don't get enough information to prepare for children in special education, and you're in a position to help.

Three Bad Reasons Not To

1. **I survived gym and my child will, too.** Think about this: If your parents had the ability back then to make things better for you, wouldn't you have wanted them to try?

2. **I'm intimidated by some gym teachers.** You and me both. Ask your child's case manager to convey the message about adherence to IEP requirements if you're too sheepish to speak.

3. **My child loves gym!** Really? Are you sure? Every minute? Every sport? Great! Still, it wouldn't hurt to have some independent verification of that, and assurance that her love for gym does not cause her to go bonkers for the rest of the day.

Keep In Mind

A paraprofessional can be a great asset to your child at gym, but make sure everybody's in agreement as to why he's there. Helping and refocusing and making sure your child doesn't get hurt are potentially good contributions; pulling your child off to the side so the teacher doesn't have to deal with her is a potentially bad one. Then again, if you're perfectly fine with the notion of your child being pulled off to the side when the activity is unsafe, make sure the aide's got something for her to do—forty minutes of boredom can also mess up the rest of the school day.

38   Learn How to Write a Good Letter

Maybe you'll never have to write a formal letter about your child's special-education program.

Let's hope not. Let's hope that the networking and volunteering, the conferencing and communication books, the e-mailing and informal chats will eliminate any need for official correspondence.

But the time may come when you need to write a good letter. It doesn't even have to be a bad time. Sometimes you'll want to confirm an understanding already discussed. Sometimes you'll want to make sure that a school employee gets credit that's due. Sometimes you'll want to file a request. And, yeah, sometimes you'll want to complain in the strongest possible way.

So write a letter. But think, first, about the best way to say what you want to say. Think about how you feel when you get an official letter from the school. Is there language that puts you on guard or puts you to sleep? Is there a letter length beyond which you skim but do not read? Keep these preferences of your own in mind when you set out to argue your case on paper.

Here's a very general template you can use in composing your own letter. Adjust it as needed for style and subject matter:

[Date]

TO: [Name of individual]

[Title of individual]

FROM: [Your name]

Parent

RE: [Your child's name]

[Your child's grade, school, placement, and any other pertinent identifying information]

Dear [Mr./Mrs./Ms.] [Last name of recipient]:

I am writing in regard to [Describe your issue, in three or four sentences. Keep rewriting this paragraph until you can get it down to just the most pertinent facts. Include any prior contacts that have been made on the subject.].

I would like to request that [Describe the outcome you are seeking here. Include any IEP agreements, legal citations, prior promises, recommendations for your child's disability, etc. Remember that special-education law only requires that services be "appropriate," not "best," so use that word when . . . appropriate.].

I will give you a call on [date about a week away] to follow up on this. Thank you for your assistance with this matter.

Sincerely,

[Your name]

[Your street address]

[Your city, state, and zip code]

[Your phone number]

[Your e-mail]

cc: [Copy the name of one person you think will make your request harder to duck, if applicable. It might be the immediate superior of the individual you're writing or a school-board member you know. I used to have some luck with cc-ing our caseworker at the state special-child health services office.]

Don't feel you need to dash this off and get it out. Do what you'd tell your child to do: Write an outline of what you want to say. Write a rough draft. Polish it up. If it's important enough to write about, it's important enough to do right.

Five Good Reasons to Do It

1. Making a written request starts the clock on obtaining services.
2. Copies of letters make good records of issues addressed.
3. They're a good opportunity to show yourself as a responsible adult.
4. Copying a letter to higher-ups often gets lower-downs moving faster.
5. It's good practice in reining in emotions for a higher purpose.

Three Bad Reasons Not To

1. **I'll just make a phone call.** Phone calls are the perfect communication method for many things. However, there will be times when you will want a written record of exactly the points you're making, so that others can't misquote you or pretend that things weren't said. A letter provides that.

2. **I'll just send an e-mail.** E-mail is quickly making written paper-based letters obsolete, but it hasn't quite done it yet. A letter in an envelope with a stamp and a signature still feels more official and weighty than an e-mail message. When your subject is weighty, too, choose a letter.

3. **I write letters all the time, and everyone ignores them.** That's why you're going to do three things: Set a date in the letter for a follow-up phone call. Copy the letter to someone at a higher level who will expect to see some results. Then, send the letter certified mail so you'll get proof that it was delivered.

Keep In Mind

Righteous indignation feels good, doesn't it? Spilling out your anger and sarcasm and spite on a piece of paper that's going to be seen by the one who done you wrong is cathartic, and it may be a necessary step for moving on. So write that letter. Get it all out. Then run it through the shredder, and write something befitting a grownup. Even if the person you're writing deserves all that bile, you don't want to have a hard-copy record of it out there in enemy hands. On the record, you're above that.

39 Stay Involved with Goings-On in Your School District

When your child is in special education, getting federally mandated services as spelled out in a legally binding IEP, it's easy to think that the workings of your local school district are not of concern to you.

Think again.

Your child's services may originate from federal law and state directives, but they have to be carried out on the local level, and that puts you at the mercy of district policies and politics. Your child's legal protections give you a little extra weight in battles with the bureaucracy, but the legal directives also gives the district the ability to throw a little weight on you, as they interpret that law to suit current controversies.

You may not have the will or the ability to fight City Hall, but you can certainly stay on top of how local issues in the schools and the community are impacting your child.

If you've done some of the things already mentioned here—started attending school events and meetings, formed conversational relationships with school personnel, spent some time volunteering and listening to nearby gossip—your job of keeping a finger on the pulse of the district will likely be done for you. You'll hear about outrages existing and coming, and you'll know where to choose your battles.

However, if you haven't hooked into that information pipeline, there are some fairly easy ways to get the scoop. School-board meetings are usually open to the public and are often broadcast on TV so you can witness all the bluster from the comfort of your couch. Keep an eye on your local paper for articles about schools, and then read the Letters to the Editor page to see what's got people hot under the collar.

And when there's an election for school board or school budget? Pay attention to the issues and the rhetoric. And vote! You have an opportunity there to stand up and be a voice for kids with special needs just by visiting a voting booth. In a time when too few citizens vote at all, much less on the local level, it doesn't take very many votes to make a difference.

Particularly at election times, but at other times throughout the year as well, your district may have informational meetings to fill parents in on what's going on with school programs and philosophies. Try to go to these if you possibly can. They will help you know of changes that you may want to protest or promote. They will give you an opportunity to stand and be recognized as an advocate for your child and children like her. And you may develop some good contacts to add to your networking. Never hurts if the higher-up you have to copy on a letter is someone who's seen you make the effort to make it to a meeting.

Five Good Reasons to Do It

1. It's easier to make a difference before something happens than after the fact.
2. As a parent and taxpayer, you have a right and responsibility to be informed.
3. So few people participate in district meetings and elections that you can make a real difference.
4. You may meet people who will be in a position to help you later.
5. Local politics has enough melodrama and scheming to qualify as reality entertainment. Think of it as *School District Survivor.*

Three Bad Reasons Not To

1. **District meetings are boring.** Yeah, they often are. And you should feel free to tune out when it's all about back-patting and -stabbing. Keep an ear open, though, for anything that might impact your child or special-education planning, including school overcrowding, teacher hiring, busing, bringing students in from out of district, and inclusion.

2. **Things are going to happen whether I get involved or not.** Maybe they will, but it never hurts for people to see that parents of children in special education speak up and stand up for their students. Too often, we get a reputation for disinterest. Change that. Be interested.

3. **I never get information about meetings.** Sometimes, when you're outside of normal information channels, it can be hard to know what's going on. Still, with a little effort, including checking newspaper listings of local events, watching your local public access station, referring to the district website, and staying in touch with people more involved than yourself, you should be able to keep tabs on events.

Keep In Mind

In many communities, matters of school policy are often argued in the Letters to the Editor section of the local paper. On those issues which you feel strongly about, consider submitting a letter of your own. The voices of special-needs families are not heard often enough, and these days chiming in is as easy as sending an e-mail.

40   Learn about Local Advocacy Groups

Sometimes it may feel like you're in this alone, doing battle as one small individual against an uncaring system.

Buck up. You've got backup.

Parent advocacy organizations may be formed on a local basis or on a statewide one, but they're likely to be great sources of information, training, empowerment, and support. And couldn't we all use some of that?

Ironically, one of the best ways to find out about advocacy groups in your area is to contact your district's special-education department. This may seem like asking the enemy to help you find extra troops, but because school districts are often mandated to increase parental participation in the process, they may help groups form, spread word of groups, or host presentations by them in an effort to do that.

You may also be able to find out about groups in your city by contacting a group in your state. The Pacer Center has a database of parent advisory groups at *www.taalliance.org/ptidirectory/index.asp,* and if you can find one in your wider area, it should be able to both provide assistance and direct you to help closer to home.

Groups like these are useful in sharing information on the way special-education law is being interpreted where you're at. There are national groups and sites and books that can give great general advice, but knowing the players and the way they play provides an important advantage. You can find out if certain services have ever been given, learn the name of a person to complain to, compare different schools and districts, and get face-to-face counseling and advice.

There's enormous comfort in realizing that you're not the only one who has been having the experiences you've been through. And, as selfish as it may seem, in realizing that as difficult as things have been, others have had it harder. You may have a piece of advice and experience that somebody needs, or be able to commiserate about a mutually frustrating situation. Parents who have gone through the same schools before you can advise on teachers to seek or avoid, administrators and their preferences, volunteer opportunities, and programs your child might be interested in. What would take you months to figure out for yourself, you can pick up in one evening.

And needless to say, if it becomes necessary to speak up about a problem, it's more effective to speak as a group, and safer-feeling, too. Often, advocacy organizations will have professional staff, or at least very experienced parents, who can lead the charge when necessary. Even if you're not in it for the rabble-rousing, though, you can learn about lots more ways to support your child's special education that are appropriate to your particular local realities.

Knowledge is power, right?

Five Good Reasons to Do It

1. Resources that would take you ages to gather yourself may be waiting for you there.
2. Parents you meet at advocacy groups may have kids who will be friend material for yours.
3. It's a good place to network for people who can help your child in school and in the community.
4. It makes you look like an active, involved parent.
5. Going to meetings can give you a much-needed night out.

Three Bad Reasons Not To

1. **It will make me look like a malcontent.** I suppose one person's active and involved is another person's malcontent. But if you wouldn't hesitate to join a professional organization or one that advocates for people in your age group or tax bracket, ask yourself: Isn't advocating for your child as important as that? It's your job, like it or not. And jobs need networking.
2. **I don't want to get involved in advocacy.** Then go to these groups for the fellowship, the support, and the information. They may or may not lead you into being a stronger advocate, but those things are valuable all by themselves.

3. **There's no group in my area.** So . . . start one. Chances are you're not the only parent who could use some company. Ask your child's teacher and case manager if they know of other parents who are looking for support, post ads in community spots and newspapers, and see who shows up. Every group has to start somewhere. Why not with you?

Keep In Mind

Right now, school seems like the only thing that matters in your child's life and future. But the time will come when school ends, and what will become of your child then? State parent-advocacy organizations often have lots of information on programs for adults with disabilities, including contacts with agencies that serve them, and meetings in which those groups can share their offerings. It may seem like you won't need this stuff for a long time, but time flies, oh dear.

41 Join an E-Mail Group for Special-Needs Parents

Having a local advisory group for face-to-face meetings and information relevant to your particular district is a valuable tool for supporting your child's special education. But sometimes it helps to have a more far-flung group of parents who can provide you with perspectives from other places and share what works for them.

It's good, when your district is saying, "That can't be done," to find out that other administrators have found a way.

It's good, too, to have people to pour your frustrations out to who you won't see later in the supermarket.

One of the many ways the Internet has been a fabulous gift to parents is in providing a platform for a wide array of forums, message boards, and e-mail lists. The latter are particularly appealing, since they provide a fairly stable group of listeners, it's easy to save good pieces of advice, and the material on them is generally not subject to search engines. A well-run list will have some precautions in place to make sure that correspondents are who they say they are and will behave themselves better than third-graders in a lunchroom.

Groups like this also give you a good opportunity to share your expertise and to help others as you have been helped. There should be a good flow of give and take among parents who are motivated to make the most of their children's education.

Yahoo Groups (*http://groups.yahoo.com*) is a good place to start looking for an e-mail group. Yahoo offers a huge number to choose from, on a variety of subjects, with a variety of group sizes. Once you've registered with Yahoo, it's easy to join and unjoin groups. Try searching for your child's particular disability, or for "special education" and a qualifying phrase like an age group or placement type. You may have to weed through a number of inappropriate offerings, but you should find one or more to suit your needs.

Family Village (*www.familyvillage.wisc.edu/library.htm*) and About.com Parenting Special Needs (*http://specialchildren.about. com/od/gettingadiagnosis/a/alphabetsoup.htm*) have e-mail groups or online support sites among their resource listings for different disabilities. These can help you find groups of parents with whom to share all aspects of your child's experience, school included.

It's easy to feel isolated when your child goes to a school outside the neighborhood, isn't included in local groups, or is misunderstood and shunned by nearby parents and kids. Remote buddies, as close as the computer and an e-mail away, may be the best way to find a community for yourself and your child. And that can make you a more confident and knowledgeable advocate when school challenges arise.

Five Good Reasons to Do It

1. Everyone needs someone to rant to.
2. Learning how it's done elsewhere can help you get things done where you are.
3. You can have fun with friends on the Net and call it research.
4. Sometimes correspondents in the same area will get together for real, and your child may meet some new friends.
5. If you don't like the way someone in the group behaves, you can just forward their missives to the trash.

Three Bad Reasons Not To

1. **I don't have a computer.** If that's for financial reasons, use the computer at the public library to set up a free online e-mail account, and use that. If it's not for financial reasons . . . oh, goodness, you really need to get one. You're not only holding yourself back from information and support, you're holding your child back from learning how to use a tool that can greatly extend his ability to complete schoolwork, do research, make friends, and become employable.

2. **I'm worried about confidentiality.** The idea of strangers having your history on their hard drives can be a little daunting. If you're concerned, set up a free online e-mail account from a service like Google or Yahoo that doesn't have

your name in the address, and be careful about providing names and specific details in your posts. There's no way to be 100 percent protected, but if you watch what you say, it's no more dangerous than talking to someone in person in a schoolyard.

3. **I can't find a group that's right for me.** So . . . start one. Just as Yahoo Groups makes it easy to join a group, it's also easy to start a group. You may find some other drifters who've been looking for a place to meet, too.

Keep In Mind

The same rule applies to e-mail as well as to more formal correspondence: It never hurts to set what you've written aside, cool down, and write it again. People on e-mail lists may get your goat, but it's rarely wise to fire back full of anger and contempt. Take a breath, and you'll be glad later.

42 Prepare a Packet on Your Child's Special Needs

You'd like to think that every teacher your child has will be an expert on her particular disability. You'd like to believe that everyone who comes in contact with him will be experienced in the proper behavior management and learning strategies. You'd like to assume that everybody has read the IEP and understands it, and that this document contains everything there is for an educator to know about your child.

You'd like to. But you shouldn't.

Chances are, your child's teacher will be an expert generally on a group of disabilities, and have some strong knowledge about certain disabilities that a larger number of kids have had, but even with all the expertise in the world, she will never know more about your child than you do.

You are the repository of specific knowledge about your child's history, strengths, and weaknesses. Also, since teachers and caseworkers and therapists come and go in your child's school life, you're the repository of all of their accumulated wisdom as well. Run with that role. Take it upon yourself at the start of the school year to pass on the information that will help the new teacher start out on the right foot, rather than taking weeks or months to figure things out.

Do that by putting together an introductory packet on your child. Write a page or two on particular strategies that have worked and things you need the teacher to know. Include some articles on your child's disability, and a copy of any behavior plans or portions of the IEP you particularly want the teacher to take note of. Make your tone one of helping, not lecturing. This is as much for the teacher's advantage as it is for your child's.

You can get some material to start your packet by finding your child's diagnosis on the list at *http://specialchildren.about.com/ od/specialeducation/a/schoolprintouts.htm* and tailoring it to your child's particular information. If you can't find an appropriate diagnosis there, try searching the Internet with terms like the diagnosis plus "information for teachers" or "school issues" or "school nurse." You may be able to turn up some good resources to share that way. Books about your child's diagnosis also often have sections on school that might be worth sharing with a teacher or case manager.

You wouldn't want a doctor to see your child without a file full of medical history to refer to. Make sure the teacher has some educational history, with your personal spin on it, as soon as work with your child begins.

Five Good Reasons to Do It

1. You get your point of view in there right away.
2. You establish yourself as a helpful and proactive parent.
3. You make sure important IEP information has been seen.
4. You save your child the stress of having a clueless teacher experience.
5. If there's a problem later, you can say you warned them.

Three Bad Reasons Not To

1. **That's the case manager's job.** Yeah, the case manager should make sure the teacher sees the IEP and fill him in on your child. And that will happen. Eventually. When things settle down and schedules get resolved. You have an opportunity to get that info out there on the first day of school, in a form you approve of, with the information you find most important. Doesn't mean the case manager can't do it, too. Later.

2. **I want the teacher to get to know my child without preconceptions.** Well, would you say, "I don't want anybody to judge what my child can and cannot do because she's deaf, so I'm not going to tell anybody she can't hear"? In that situation, you'd recognize that, while preconceptions are to be guarded against, there's some basic information that needs to be understood so your child can be safe at school

and participate fully. The exact same thing is true for behavioral and developmental and mental-health and "invisible" medical disabilities. Why would you want someone taking care of your child who doesn't know the first thing about keeping him safe?

3. **It's the teacher's job to know this.** And it's a parent's job to know how to parent, yet you appreciate help and information and ideas and inspiration. Don't deny the person in charge of your child's schooling that advantage, too.

Keep In Mind

Note that what we're talking about here is a packet, not an encyclopedia. Resist the urge to include every article and every milestone and every last thing you can think of. Make it too weighty, and the teacher will never read it. You want to get the most important information up front, support it with a few helpful and easy-to-read articles, and offer to meet for more detailed information exchange. Give help, but have mercy.

43 Write a Positive Student Profile on Your Child

When you're putting together material to give to your child's teacher, the things you think of tend to be the negative ones. Do this when his behavior gets out of control. Do that to accommodate her reading problems. Use this tool to help him hear you. Use that strategy to help her pay attention.

Like it or not, kids are in special education because of what they can't do. IEPs address deficits. Our encounters with teachers generally occur when there's a problem in the classroom. Meetings with caseworkers and administrators are rarely called to talk about how well a student is doing.

As a parent, you're in the best position to see the complete picture of your child, the good as well as the bad, the strengths as well as the weaknesses. You've been watching that picture grow deeper and more colorful over the years, and you are its foremost interpreter. So while it's important to make sure that teachers know how to handle your child's problems in the most proactive and useful way, it's also important to make sure the problem is not the only thing they see.

A good way to convey that message is with a Positive Student Profile.

The Statewide Parent Advocacy Network of New Jersey has a great template of a student profile on its site at *www.spannj.org/BasicRights/appendix_c.htm*, along with some samples filled out to give you an idea of how to proceed. You start by listing who your child is—a brother, a SpongeBob fan, a key collector, a ballet student—then list strengths and successes before getting to challenges and supports needed. The profile ends with a description of your dreams for your child (you do have some of those, right?) and a space for additional information.

A student profile such as this, filled out with care and thoughtfulness and, maybe, a sense of humor, is the perfect thing to put on top of the packet we talked about giving teachers in the previous chapter. It puts your child's best foot forward, while still reinforcing the need for accommodations, modifications, and special handling. It also lets teachers know, right off the bat, that this student has parents who think she's terrific, and who support all the aspects of her life and education.

Five Good Reasons to Do It

1. It counters the negativity of so much of the paperwork on your child.
2. It gets you focused on thinking of positive things to say about your child.

3. It helps the teacher see your child as a three-dimensional human being.
4. It gives the teacher things to talk to your child about.
5. It provides a great introduction to that information packet you're going to give the teacher.

Three Bad Reasons Not To

1. **The teacher doesn't want all this paper.** The teacher doesn't want a novel. The teacher doesn't want another incredibly thick file that he doesn't have time to read. The teacher doesn't want paragraph upon paragraph of closely typed ranting about the way your child has been treated and the way she's really brilliant and misunderstood. But a clearly presented, easy to follow, upbeat and helpful profile of a new student? Most teachers would say thanks for that.

2. **The IEP paints a pretty good picture of my child.** How lucky for you! You have a good team that understands your kid, and you've been able to provide some input to make it an effective tool. Still, write that profile, and send it in on Day 1. Your child's teacher may not have received the IEP or may not have had time to go over it in detail. A quick introduction never hurts, and it will reinforce your caring and thoughtfulness as a parent.

3. **I can't think of a single positive thing to say.** Certainly, we all have days like that. Weeks. Months. But even kids with serious issues, who make things very difficult at home, have strengths. Think of how the things that drive you crazy may reflect abilities like verbal cleverness, manual dexterity, ability to focus on a task, or creativity. Brainstorm with a family member if it helps you to recognize those things about your child that are worthy of recognition.

Keep In Mind

A Positive Student Profile is a good thing to send in on the first day of school, but if you're reading this midyear, it's not too late to go ahead and fill one out—especially if you haven't been communicating much with the teacher. Just send it with a note explaining that you saw the idea and thought it would be worthwhile to share your observations. You'll give the teacher a renewed interest in your child and some additional things to talk about.

44   Read Your Child's IEP

It's not exactly light reading, is it? That thick packet of educational jargon, full of incomprehensible testing information and goals worded in a way that ensures parents won't be able to figure out what they are, is a pretty intimidating piece of work. It's completely understandable if what you most want to do with it is shove it in a file cabinet and never think of it again.

Still: Read it. Do a page a day, if that helps, or one small section. Read it aloud to your spouse. Bring it on bus rides or other spots where reading is better than nothing. You don't have to enjoy it, or even "get" all of it, but you do need to read it.

It details all of the hard work your child is going to have to do, and the people charged with educating your child are going to have to do. What does it say if you're not willing to do a little hard work, too?

Here are some things to look for as you carve your way through that mighty document:

- ▶ Are there any really obvious or glaring errors? I've seen IEPs that had the wrong gender for the child, and even the wrong name. Often boilerplate information is cut-and-pasted between IEPs, and accidents happen.

- Do the descriptions sound like my child? The first page or two should have some semi-decipherable text about your child's level of achievement, personal history, and specific challenges. If what you read there does not sound like the child you know, flag it for discussion. Even if it does turn out to be an accurate reflection of teacher and examiner observations, you can always add your own parent statement to provide an opposing viewpoint.

- Do the goals seem appropriate? You don't have to get too much into the nitty-gritty of percentages and repetitions and measurable-ness and what-all if you don't want to. Just look for things that have been set as goals that your child already does. If simple addition is a math goal and your kid's been doing that on homework for a year, ask why it's still hanging out there.

- Can you work on the goals at home? Sometimes, teachers provide extra information in the goals for home reinforcement; if not, look for a few things where you can figure out some home practice, and try it out.

- Are any services missing? Make sure things like therapy, bus transportation, paraprofessional help, accommodations, and modifications are specifically mentioned in the document. If not, sound the alarm.

Five Good Reasons to Do It

1. You can catch typos and easy-to-fix errors that the folks in charge don't have time to check for.

2. You'll become more familiar with your child's educational program.

3. You'll have some points for discussion at the next IEP meeting.

4. You'll avoid lost services by catching missing items.

5. All that paper was used up on you; it's your obligation to the trees to at least give it a look.

Three Bad Reasons Not To

1. **It's too confusing.** Yes. It is. But I wonder: What do you do when your child gives that as an excuse not to read or try something? Maybe you point out that it's important to challenge yourself, and that hard work stretches your brain and makes it work better, or that you'll never know what you can do until you try. Use those same strategies on yourself.

2. **I didn't get a copy.** Well, that's a problem. The school district is legally required to give you one, and to let you read it before you sign. If it's gone astray, inquire about that immediately. And if you had one and it got misplaced, ask politely for another.

3. **I'm afraid I'll find something bad.** Chances are, if there's a problem with your district or your team, you already know it. Not reading about it won't fix it, but it will keep you from having any chance at doing so. What's more likely, though, is that you'll find small unintended errors that the human beings who put the plan together missed.

Keep In Mind

The best time to read your child's IEP is before you sign it. But if you didn't do that—if you signed before reading because you were strong-armed or you wanted to be cooperative or there were no areas of dispute that worried you—don't beat yourself up about it. Just go ahead and read it now. It's never too late to ask questions and make changes. You can always get a benefit from working on the goals offered there with your child; and you'll have something to talk about at teacher meetings and that next IEP get-together.

45 Meet with Your Planning Team Outside of IEP Season

Don't be a stranger! That's good advice when you want to establish any relationship, whether it's with neighbors or acquaintances or prospective play-date pals for your child. And it's appropriate to think about when you're trying to establish a relationship with the school personnel who hold your child's IEP fate in their hands. Don't let that super-tense once-a-year meeting be the only time you lay eyes on each other.

Aside from the teacher and therapists, who you're already making regular contact with, your IEP team will generally consist of a school psychologist, learning consultant, and social worker. You may be assigned one of them as your case manager for a particular reason, or just due to luck of the draw.

If you don't know the names of all these team members and couldn't pick them out of a line-up, stop by their office and introduce yourself. It doesn't hurt to check in at the start of the school year, too, and make sure that the same team is in place as the one you left at the end of the last school year. Staff often gets shuffled around without prompt announcement, and meeting the new workers and welcoming them to the school can help them get to know your child much more quickly.

For parents who volunteer in school (which should be you), it's easy enough to just drop by the office informally without making a big deal about it. Other good opportunities to stop in are at back-to-school nights when all school personnel are on hand, or after a teacher conference. Once you know what everybody looks like, you may notice team members at school activities and be able to have informal conversations with them there.

If it's not easy to speak in person, give a call to your case manager every so often to ask about something, to recommend a service you've found useful, or to talk about how your child is doing. Remember the team members in your holiday baked-good distributions or end-of-year thank-you notes, particularly if they've been helpful to you on an issue in dispute. You don't want to be a nuisance, but you don't want to be . . . well, a stranger, either.

Think about how aggravating it is when some mystery person from the district comes to your IEP meeting and expects to be an important part of the process, when you barely know the name. Don't you be that sort of mystery person, then, yourself. Building a rapport now will make things so much less scary later.

Five Good Reasons to Do It
1. IEP meetings will be less stressful if you have friends around the table.

2. You'll have a better chance of getting information when you need it.
3. Get a friendly relationship going, and you may hear good gossip about what's going on in the school and the district.
4. You can insert your point of view in a nonadversarial environment.
5. Your presence reinforces the fact that your child has a caring advocate going to some trouble for his interests.

Three Bad Reasons Not To

1. **They're always too busy for me.** Don't break up a meeting when you go to the team office, and be sensitive if the members look harried. Start with a simple hi, and if you don't get invited further, at least you tried.
2. **The team is not located at my child's school.** That lets out informal face-to-face meetings, but phone calls and e-mails are still entirely good to do. Find a reason to check in every now and again.
3. **Those people intimidate me.** If the only time you ever see your team members is in the heightened atmosphere of an IEP meeting, then they always will. And true, if you stop by or call, you may initially get the same stiffness. Again, you're not trying to be best friends or impose yourself. Just trying to show yourself between meetings. Take a deep breath and do it.

Keep In Mind

Meeting informally with teachers and therapists and team members throughout the school year is a great way to support your child's special education between IEP meetings. But first and foremost, do go to the IEP meeting. You may not feel equipped to advocate or propose or debate or evaluate or do anything other than sit there, but you can sit there. Put your behind on that seat. Students whose parents do not participate in the IEP process stand a good chance of missing out on services and special considerations because nobody is standing up for them, and everybody knows it. Even without words, your presence can speak volumes. There's time to grow into the advocacy portion; if you're not at that point yet, just focus on the attendance portion.

46 Be Clear about Your Own Goals for Your Child

What do you want for your child? What do you see her doing as an adult? What level of education do you imagine he'll attain? What degree of independence do you think is realistic?

Do you let yourself ask those questions? In some ways, it may be best not to. It's easy to allow dreams of the future to rule every present interaction, and there's a lot to be said for enjoying your child where your child is at right now.

But as you look at your child's educational program, at the type of classroom she's in and the pace of the instruction he's receiving, it's worth thinking about whether it leads to a place that you want your child to go. If not, discuss it with the IEP team. They may have their own goals and expectations, and it will benefit you to hear them. Maybe they will help you see your child the way they do. Or maybe they will help you realize that you need to convey more clearly why you see your child differently.

You'll have to be willing to support those goals with your own time and effort. If you want your child to have a full education, don't be complaining about homework. If you see your child as being independent one day, work to find ways to teach organization and life skills. It's easy to get caught up in the desire for help and accommodation, but they should be in the service of getting your child where she needs to be, not keeping her where she's at.

Your child's IEP is chock-full of important sounding goals. These are short-term goals, to be accomplished within the school year. Consider developing some goals of your own for the same period of time, covering things you want your child to accomplish at home or in life. Share your goals with teachers and therapists, because support for that effort may be folded into the work being done at school, just as you support school goals at home.

Five Good Reasons to Do It

1. You'll have something hopeful to work on with your child.
2. Making goals helps you see what needs to be done now and in the future.
3. Goals offer a good opportunity for collaboration with school personnel.
4. Discussing goals with school personnel ensures that you're all working toward the same ends.
5. You get a sense of accomplishment when goals are met.

Three Bad Reasons Not To

1. **I don't want to stress out my child.** So don't set goals that are too hard. IEP goals are meant to be measurable and practical; make sure the ones you set are as well, and rig them toward your child's success. If your child is really struggling, take a big goal and break it into tiny steps. Give lots of positive feedback when each step is attained. A good book to help you teach life skills this way is *Steps to Independence: Teaching Everyday Skills to Children with Special Needs* by Bruce L. Baker and Alan J. Brightman.

2. **My child has enough goals at school.** Chances are, you have goals at work that need to be met each workday or pay period or year. Yet once you get home, you may still set yourself goals that have to do with things around the household or with your child's school situation. Different goals for different locales are something that most people set. Your child should be no different. Working for something is a positive experience no matter where you do it.

3. **I'm afraid I'll set my goals too low.** What happens when you look toward the future and see not much of one? It's hard to get motivated to set goals when there's nothing very appealing waiting at the other end. You want to avoid being overly ambitious and setting your child up for long-term failure, but don't be afraid of small successes, either. If the

far-off vision is too discouraging, set small goals for what your child can do right now, today. You may be surprised how far small steps can take you.

Keep In Mind

There may be goals that you don't want to pursue for your child at any given time. For example, independence is a goal that is often stressed in schools, particularly as students move into middle and high school. But for some children with behavioral or developmental special needs, independence granted too early can be dangerous. It may be better to work hard on other goals that lay a better foundation for future independence, but you'll have to argue that case with the school based on your own experience and research on your child's disability. Having a safe and successful year is a worthy goal, too.

47   Make Peace with the Need for Help

I remember a conversation I had with a fellow parent a number of years ago whose daughter had been offered resource-room instruction in reading. The mom, while acknowledging that her child was struggling, was resistant to seeking that extra help, because it might keep the girl from getting into Harvard one day.

I don't know if Harvard was any sort of realistic goal for this particular child, but I think there is a danger in keeping your eyes so strongly on the long-term prospects that you miss the opportunity to give your child what's needed right now.

Often, it's a matter of solving smaller problems now instead of tackling bigger problems later. Services provided in preschool and elementary school can set a solid foundation to build on. It's like the difference between taking your car to the mechanic when the warning light comes on and waiting until you're stranded at the side of the road with a burned-out engine. The effectiveness of the intervention and the likelihood of making a complete recovery get less the longer you wait.

When your child has an "invisible disability," it can be hard to accept that help is something that's absolutely necessary. Try thinking of it as similar to a more noticeable disability. You might accept that a physically handicapped student needs a ramp to get up some stairs, or a hearing-impaired student needs a sign-language interpreter. In just the same way, a behavior-challenged child needs a good behavior plan, and a learning-disabled student needs accommodations that help her learn. The sooner you make peace with that, the sooner your child can start getting the assistance he needs, and the more quickly, perhaps, he will need less of it.

There will be enough people in your child's life who will question the aid that's given. You, your child's cheerleader, the interface between your child and school, should be the spokesperson for appropriate support and help. Listen, really listen to your child, and don't let aspirations that don't fit keep her from services that do. That's not helping, and help should be your job, too.

Five Good Reasons to Do It

1. Your child needs to know you're looking to protect his interests, not your ambitions.

2. A disagreement on the amount of assistance needed can get between you and a productive relationship with your child's teacher.

3. Sometimes, people who work directly with your child at school will see a greater need in some areas than you see at home.

4. The earlier help is given, the more painless it is to provide it and receive it.

5. You'll avoid any guilty feeling your child may have if she senses you disagree with her needs.

Three Bad Reasons Not To

1. **Getting help makes you needy.** Tell that to the person who's drowning and needs a life preserver. Sometimes, help is what keeps you afloat. You have to draw a difference between smothering a child with help and giving him the tools needed to succeed. There's no way to justify denying the latter.

2. **The school wants to give too much help.** That happens. Ask why. What are they seeing that makes their opinion so much different from yours. Do they understand your child's disability? Are they are aware of her history? Do they know of techniques other districts are using? The research and rapport you've been gaining throughout this book pay off here. Don't resent, don't deny. Ask.

3. **I don't want my child to feel different.** Well, the ship's already sailed on that, hasn't it? Your child isn't different because he needs help, he needs help because he's different. Not giving that help doesn't make him less different, it makes him more different. Of course, "different" is only a

bad thing if you make it one, by conveying that it's shameful to need the things he needs. With more and more kids getting services these days, Harvard should be pretty understanding about it by the time your child hits college age. You should be, too.

Keep In Mind

Always keep in mind that, though you may have all sorts of research and ideas and theories of what will be best for your child, you are not the person who has to sit through the class and experience the difficulties and suffer from being pushed too hard. I was all for having my daughter in an inclusion class for reading, until I saw the toll that the stress of being in a too-challenging environment was taking on her. Whether or not it was the best thing for her education, it was disastrous for her emotional life. I had to back off and let the help and the healing begin. Her program is less ambitious, but she's much happier, and I'm relieved.

48   Make Peace with the Need for Advocacy

So you're fine with your child getting services. You're totally at peace with it. The school has your blessing to do whatever seems appropriate for your child. Just as long as you don't have to be involved.

That's a perfectly understandable philosophy. Advocacy is hard. It involves know-it-alls with fancy degrees yelling at you. It involves threats to your child's well-being and to your sanity. It's not fun. But it's absolutely vital.

No, you don't have to scorch the earth at IEP meetings. You don't have to come to school with a team of lawyers, ready to do battle. It's not necessary to tear the IEP apart looking for trouble or debate the righteousness of every grade.

All you have to do is stand up for your child and let everybody know you care.

That involves, first and foremost, the kind of things we've been talking about in this book. Forming relationships with teachers and therapists and case managers. Being involved in the life of the school. Doing research and preparing it in a way that helps the teacher. These are actions that say, "My child has somebody on his side."

You'd be shocked by how many children have nobody. And while school personnel may feel protective of those kids and feel bad for them, the fact is, now and always, that the squeaky wheel gets the grease. The kid whose mother is around, whom everybody knows, who gets support at home and brings support to school, is likely to get better help and more leeway

If you disagree with something that's going on, you'll be in a position to talk about it without having to argue about it. You can decide, based on your knowledge of the people involved, whether you need to really push the issue or it will settle itself. You can provide ideas and materials that can help resolve the matter agreeably. And if you have to pull some weight, the team members will know that you are doing it from an involved and informed place and not arbitrarily, and that can help cooler heads prevail.

Nobody wants to fight, even the people who do it. There are different types and levels and heats of advocacy. The only kind of advocacy that's undesirable is no advocacy at all. Be a voice for your child.

Five Good Reasons to Do It
1. Positive advocacy brings benefits to you and your child.
2. Your advocacy will keep your child from being lost in the system.
3. Being a proactive part of the process can keep problems from starting.

4. You may find that you knew more about these issues than you thought.
5. You'll feel better about yourself if you're standing up for your child.

Three Bad Reasons Not To

1. **I don't know anything about this school stuff.** But you know everything about this child. Your expertise in your child's history makes you A-one prime advocate material.
2. **The school doesn't want me to be an advocate.** The school doesn't want you coming to meetings with an attitude and an agenda. They shouldn't mind you wanting to be a concerned and active parent. Most special educators I speak to lament the lack of involvement of an appreciable number of parents. Don't be one of those.
3. **Advocates are too expensive.** Hiring an advocate can be expensive, both financially and emotionally. We're not talking about that level of advocacy. We're just talking about the school knowing that a student has involved and supportive parents who are interested in working collaboratively for the success of all. That good rapport is absolutely free.

Keep In Mind

Even with the best efforts of committed educators, there are things that fall through the cracks in a special-education program—therapy that's not provided, in-class help that never shows up, accommodations that aren't communicated. Without your advocacy, that may never get caught and fixed. Though school officials may wince at the arrival of strong advocate parents, to a large degree they are part of what keeps the system running smoothly and responsibly. If you're not doing that job, your child is not the only one you're letting down.

49   Set Some Goals for Yourself

You've set some goals for your child, and so has the school. But why stop there? Goals are good for organization, prioritization, and measuring progress. So why not set some goals for your own increased advocacy and special-education support, too?

As with your child, the goals don't have to be huge or high-minded. They should be down-to-earth and measurable. Once you feel the confidence and sense of accomplishment that comes with meeting a modest goal or two, you can begin to expand into more ambitious territory. Fail at something big right off the bat, though, and you may never get going again.

This book offers plenty of good goals to get you started. Choose one, and go for it. Or pick one to focus on each week, or each month. Choose a broader goal such as "organization" or "home-work" or "relationships with school personnel," and use the chapters that deal with those issues to motivate and guide you. Don't begin with chores you dread or fear. Remember that the most important thing is getting started, and you want to do something that makes that simple.

One goal might be to touch base with one teacher or thera-pist or administrator a month; write these down in your contact log and realize how much more you're doing than you were doing before. Set a goal of putting in one volunteer session a month, and enjoy the increase in insight it gives you. Set a goal of one hour a night of homework help with your child, and appreciate the improvement this makes in her performance and your understanding of her schoolwork.

You know the areas in which you most need to improve your game. You also know that things aren't going to change overnight. You've been doing things the way you have been for a long time, for reasons that have to do with your schedule and your personality and your family code. Those things don't change easily, just as your child's special needs don't melt away with just a little help. But it's important to try, it's important to move, and it's important to reach goals. So set some.

You may want to share with your child's teacher or other school personnel what your goal is, and why you're trying to increase your involvement in that area. They may be able to tell you of other good opportunities for improving input in a way that will most help your child and earn you Brownie points. With so many parents doing so little to support their children's special education, you might as well get yourself a little appreciation for not being one of them.

Five Good Reasons to Do It

1. Goals are a good way to get yourself started.
2. They're also a good way to measure how far you've come.

3. Pursuing challenging goals will give you something in common with your child.
4. Sharing your goals will make you look like a conscientious parent.
5. You're going to give yourself a nice reward at the end, right?

Three Bad Reasons Not To

1. **I don't need to do anything that formal.** Well, then you're a better person than me. I find that just sort of figuring I'll do something results in something just sort of not getting done. Formalize your intentions, and it's a lot harder to duck them.
2. **I'm afraid I'll fail.** Take a trick from goal-setting for kids and make sure to select goals that are easy to achieve, even goals you are already in the process of achieving. We're not going for an advocacy marathon here, just some gentle steps in the right direction.
3. **None of the goals here fit me.** If you really, truly can't find anything in this book that reflects a need in your child's school experience, then come up with something of your own. You live with your child's schooling and its effects every day. What are the areas that most trouble you? What could you do about them? Set a goal, and go after it.

Keep In Mind

One good goal to set for yourself might be learning more about your child's school, particularly if it's outside your neighborhood and your general circle of experience. Start by taking the quiz at http://specialchildren. about.com/od/schoolissues/a/knowyourschool.htm. Can you identify these school employees? Would you be able to chat with them if you saw them at the supermarket? Would you know their names to write a note? Think about making a goal out of increasing your school IQ over the course of the school year. Make a game of it. Involve your child in filling you in about the people and places that make up his weekday world. Your child will enjoy being the expert for a change.

50   Enjoy Your Child's School Days

You're laughing at me now, aren't you. *Enjoy* these days? After I've been talking about homework and conferences and correspondence and volunteer work and IEPs and all manner of worrisome tasks?

I'm not saying you have to enjoy everything you do. But enjoy these days overall. Enjoy your child. Find ways to have fun together, even within the context of school activities and reinforcements.

If you're a good parent, you'll want your child to enjoy school. That doesn't mean she should be in permanent recess, or he should get to chat with his friends all day. Just that school should be a positive place, a place your child wants to go, and a place where things happen that she is delighted to tell you about at the end of the day.

You need to share that delight and excitement. You need to let your child know that school is a place you find interesting and worth engaging with, and let your child's teachers know that you value their work and appreciate their efforts to make school an upbeat place.

When you or your child are not enjoying things, ask yourself why. Then ask your contacts at school. Maybe the problem is too much homework or a too-long bus ride. Maybe the school routine is being disrupted, or a bully is wreaking havoc. Maybe you've lost touch with the school personnel you need to keep you up on things, and your child is feeling lost. Use a lack of enjoyment as a sign that something is not right, and work to correct it so that your child doesn't dread going to class.

School is a big deal in your child's life right now. It's his work, his play, his social circle. It should be an equally big and important part of your life. No child is really equipped to go through the school experience completely on her own, but children with special educational needs in particular require guidance and assistance and watching. The consequences of bad school experiences fall much more heavily on your family than it does on the school. You have an enormous interest in keeping those experiences positive. Your child's future—and by extension, your own—will depend on it.

It's possible for parents to get overinvested in school, to almost take over the school experience from their kids. You'll want to try to avoid that. But overinvestment, even with all its problems, is far preferable to noninvestment. Get involved. Stay interested. You'll support your child's special education, and if things work out right, you'll enjoy yourself, too.

Five Good Reasons to Do It
1. Your enthusiasm will rub off on your child.
2. Your lack of enthusiasm will also rub off, so avoid it.

3. School will be a more positive experience for your child and for his teacher, too.

4. These are the experiences and memories you will have to look back on when your child grows up; make them good ones.

5. It's better than kicking yourself for doing nothing.

Three Bad Reasons Not To

1. **I hate all of this.** Hate it! Well, bravo for doing it anyway. If you truly can't enjoy these school days, then you'll have to do what's second best: Act like you enjoy it. Don't let your child think that helping her and participating in her schooling is an excruciating experience for you. Fake it until you make it.

2. **School isn't for enjoying, it's for learning.** Honestly, there's no reason it can't be both. If you had a bad experience yourself, it may be hard to accept that. But particularly for your child with special needs, who may react very badly to stress and negative reinforcement and react very well to routine and positive reinforcement, happiness is a pretty necessary element of the day. Your happiness, too.

3. **The school keeps trying to make sure I don't enjoy myself.** If you've done some of the work in this book to form positive relationships, and you still feel that way, you have some

more work to do. Maybe it involves getting your child into a different school. Acceptance of negativity is a lousy option, for both you and your child.

Keep In Mind

Teaching techniques have changed quite a lot in recent years, with recognition that maybe rote learning done in a punitive environment is not the best thing for young brains. You may see teachers playing games, using art supplies, giving rewards, and trying other tactics that look like they're going too easy on the kiddies. However you feel about this educational trend in general, give thanks that our special kids are living in a time when it's become the norm. Whether low-stress, high-reward education is best for all kids, it's most likely resoundingly better for special-education students. And their parents.

Appendix A

Recommended Reading on Disabilities

You can find my reviews of books on a variety of specific disabilities on the About.com Parenting Special Needs site at *http://special children.about.com/od/gettingadiagnosis/a/bookreviews.htm*. The more general titles listed here have information that will help you understand and accept your child's special needs, and find joy in your life together.

Building a Joyful Life with Your Child Who Has Special Needs by Nancy J. Whiteman and Linda Roan-Yager. Journal exercises to help you find your way to acceptance and joy.

The Child with Special Needs: Encouraging Intellectual and Emotional Growth by Stanley I. Greenspan, MD, and Serena Wieder, PhD, with Robin Simons; and *The Challenging Child: Understanding, Raising, and Enjoying the Five "Difficult" Types of Children* by Stanley I. Greenspan, MD, with Jacqueline Salmon. Greenspan's my parenting guru, and he has great information about helping our special kids, presented in a positive way.

The Explosive Child: A New Approach for Understanding and Parenting Easily Frustrated, Chronically Inflexible Children by Ross W. Greene, PhD. If your child has you at the end of your rope, this book will reel you back in.

Kids in the Syndrome Mix of ADHD, LD, Asperger's, Tourette's, Bipolar and More by Martin L. Kutscher, MD. Learn how all that alphabet soup gets sorted out.

More Than a Mom: Living a Full and Balanced Life When Your Child Has Special Needs by Amy Baskin and Heather Fawcett. Guidance for all aspects of your life as a parent.

Parenting with Positive Behavior Support by Meme Hieneman, Karen Childs, and Jane Sergay. The same techniques the school should be using with your child can work at home, too.

A Parent's Guide to Developmental Delays: Recognizing and Coping with Missed Milestones in Speech, Movement, Learning, and Other Areas by Laurie LeComer. A parent-friendly look at the kinds of problems that may land your child in special education in the first place.

The Parent's Guide to Speech and Language Problems: Real-World Advice on Making Sense of Your Child's Diagnosis; Being Your Child's Best Advocate; Helping Your Child—and Your Family—Cope by

Debbie Feit with Heidi Feldman, MD. Read it before those meetings with the speech therapist.

The Special Needs Planning Guide: How to Prepare for Every Stage of Your Child's Life by John W. Nadworny and Cynthia R. Haddad. Another goal for you: Get your paperwork and your plans in order.

Steps to Independence: Teaching Everyday Skills to Children with Special Needs by Bruce L. Baker and Alan J. Brightman. Great advice for teaching life skills.

Supportive Parenting: Becoming an Advocate for Your Child with Special Needs by Jan Starr Campito. A parent explains how she became her child's biggest supporter.

Transforming the Difficult Child: The Nurtured Heart Approach by Howard Glasser, MA, and Jennifer Easley, MA. The best behavioral approach I've found for kids who respond poorly to traditional discipline.

Understanding Your Child's Puzzling Behavior: A Guide for Parents of Children with Behavioral, Social, and Learning Challenges by Steven E. Curtis, PhD. Plenty of forms to fill out to guide you toward a reasonable explanation.

Appendix B

Good Books on IEP Planning and Advocacy

Autism: Asserting Your Child's Right to a Special Education by David A. Sherman. Though it's intended for families of children with autism, there's advice here that's useful for any special-education parent.

Believe in My Child with Special Needs! Helping Children Achieve Their Potential in School by Mary A. Falvey. The author is a cheerleader for full inclusion, and she may make you one, too.

How Well Does Your IEP Measure Up? Quality Indicators for Effective Service Delivery by Diane Twachtman-Cullen and Jennifer Twachtman-Reilly. It's really more about creating an IEP that measures up rather than reviewing a current IEP, but that's plenty useful, too.

IDEA 2004: Individuals with Disabilities Education Improvement Act: A Parent Handbook for School Age Children with Learning Disabilities by Shelley Smith. A parent shares what she's learned about the law.

A Parent's Guide to Special Education: Insider Advice on How to Navigate the System and Help Your Child Succeed by Linda Wilmshurst and Alan W. Brue. Two school psychologists explain it all for you.

Wrightslaw: Special Education Law, 2nd Edition, and *Wrightslaw: From Emotions to Advocacy, 2nd Edition*, both by Peter W. D. Wright and Pamela Darr Wright. Their website, *www.wrightslaw.com*, is an essential online resource.

Appendix C

Where to Buy Therapy Equipment

Watch out, because if you start getting these therapy catalogs, you're going to want to buy everything, and much of it is priced for schools and not individuals. Still, they're great fun to look at, they may give you some ideas, and some of the items are affordable enough to use with your child or donate to the school.

From the sites listed, you can either order online or request a catalog.

Abilitations
www.abilitations.com

OT Ideas
www.otideas.com

Sensory Comfort
www.sensorycomfort.com

Southpaw Enterprises
www.southpawenterprises.com

Special Kids Zone

www.specialkidszone.com

The Speech Bin

www.speechbin.com

Therapro

www.theraproducts.com

Index

211

About the Author

Terri Mauro is the About.com guide to Parenting Special Needs Children (*http://specialchildren.about.com*) and the author of *The Everything® Parent's Guide to Sensory Integration Disorder.* Her humorous website, Mothers with Attitude at *www.motherswith attitude.com/home.html*, on which she has shared many of her special-education strategies and struggles, was named a *USA Today* Hot Site and a *Good Housekeeping* Site of the Day. Terri serves on her school district's special-education parent advisory committee, and has been trained to help other parents through the IEP process. She also has more than a dozen years experience shepherding her own two children through the special-education system.